▪▪▪▪ BRIEF CONTENTS

TABLE OF CONTENTS

▪▪▪▪▪ PREFACE

Test drive Visual Basic .NET! You may like the way it handles. *Microsoft Visual Basic .NET: Programs to Accompany Programming Logic and Design* offers a way to try out Visual Basic .NET without devoting a whole course to the endeavor.

This textbook is intended to be a companion to Joyce Farrell's textbook, *Programming Logic and Design, Third Edition* (Boston: Course Technology, 2004) and is not a stand-alone tutorial. Its goal is not so much to teach Visual Basic .NET as it is to provide hands-on activities for beginning programmers as they assimilate the concepts presented in *Programming Logic and Design*. Consequently, this textbook makes no attempt to make students proficient VB .NET programmers. Instead, it endeavors to move the ideas out of the Farrell textbook into a computer, and out of pseudocode into Visual Basic code. The author believes that this approach offers a richer introduction to programming than either book alone could provide.

This textbook, like the Farrell textbook, assumes no programming language experience. The writing is non-technical and emphasizes good programming practices. The practice activities and examples are based on those in *Programming Logic and Design*. The main difference between the two textbooks is in the computer language used: In this textbook, Visual Basic .NET syntax is used rather than pseudocode.

Visual Basic .NET is an object-oriented event-driven language. As such, it is an ideal tool for creating interactive programs, where the user is given control over what the program does. On the other hand, *Programming Logic and Design* takes a procedural approach to programming, where the computer is given a data-processing task and simply does it, from beginning to end, without user intervention. Because the purpose of this textbook is to use Visual Basic .NET to implement the data-processing tasks described in *Programming Logic and Design*, many of the topics one would expect to see in an introductory Visual Basic textbook are omitted. For example, there is very little in this textbook about objects, properties, and events. Consequently, more space can be devoted to the coding of data-processing algorithms.

ORGANIZATION AND COVERAGE

Microsoft Visual Basic .NET: Programs to Accompany Programming Logic and Design is divided into nine chapters and includes five appendices. After an introductory first chapter, the textbook corresponds to specific chapters in the Farrell textbook, as shown in the following table.

Microsoft Visual Basic .NET: Programs to Accompany Programming Logic and Design	Programming Logic and Design, Third Edition
Chapter 1: Getting Started	Not Applicable
Chapter 2: Modifying a Solution	Chapters 1–4: 1. An Overview of Computers and Logic 2. Understanding Structure 3. Modules, Hierarchy Charts, and Documentation 4. Writing and Designing a Complete Program
Chapter 3: Reading a Record	Chapters 1–4
Chapter 4: Reading a File	Chapters 1–4
Chapter 5: Modularizing a Solution	Chapters 1–4
Chapter 6: Making Decisions	Chapter 5: Making Decisions
Chapter 7: Exploring Loops	Chapter 2: Understanding Structure Chapter 6: Looping
Chapter 8: Exploring Arrays	Chapter 8: Arrays
Chapter 9: Merging Sequential Files	Chapter 11: Sequential File Merging, Matching, and Updating (Comprehensive Edition only)

Here's a closer look at the chapters in this textbook:

- Chapter 1 introduces students to Microsoft Visual Studio .NET. For the practice activities, students examine and run a Visual Basic .NET solution.

- Chapter 2 describes how to copy and modify an existing solution. For the practice activities, students navigate the Microsoft Integrated Development Environment as they debug a solution.

- Chapter 3 introduces the processing of sequential files. For the practice activities, students use Notepad to examine a sequential file and then use Visual Basic to open and close the file.

- Chapter 4 presents the data-processing paradigm discussed in *Programming Logic and Design* and relates it to Visual Basic .NET. For the practice activities, students use a WHILE loop to read a file.

- Chapter 5 modularizes a solution. For the practice activities, students write general procedures and pass arguments to procedures and functions.

- Chapter 6 describes how to use Visual Basic .NET to code the decisions discussed in *Programming Logic and Design*, Chapter 5. For the practice activities, students create reports using the information from sequential files.

- Chapter 7 explores the three kinds of loops introduced in *Programming Logic and Design*, Chapters 2 and 6. For the practice activity, students code a nested loop described in *Programming Logic and Design*, Chapter 6.

- Chapter 8 deals with arrays. For the practice activity, students use a case structure to implement the program described in *Programming Logic and Design*, Chapter 7.

- Chapter 9 merges sequential files and creates a new file for output. The chapter encompasses the same general topics as does Chapter 11 in the Comprehensive Edition of the Farrell textbook. Students who use the Comprehensive Edition of *Programming Logic and Design* will get the most from this chapter; however, the chapter is complete in itself, and reading *Programming Logic and Design*, Chapter 11 is not a prerequisite for working through this chapter.

- Five appendices provide special information about the Windows environment, such as duplicating folders, printing documents, and storing files:

  Appendix A: Duplicating a Solution Folder
  Appendix B: Printing a Form
  Appendix C: Storage of Data Files
  Appendix D: Using Reporter to Complete Exercises in This Textbook
  Appendix E: File Name Extensions

FEATURES OF THE TEXT

Every chapter in this textbook includes the following features. These features not only facilitate learning in the classroom but also enable students to learn the material at their own pace.

- Objectives: Each chapter begins with a list of objectives that orients the students to the topics that will be presented in the chapter. In addition to providing a quick reference to the topics covered, this feature provides a useful study aid.

- Figures: The figures depict actual screen shots, display explanatory tables, and provide guided "walk through" code. The visuals and examples enhance students' understanding by providing a more robust learning experience.

- Practice activities: Guided step-by-step practice activities throughout each chapter help students to reinforce the concepts being learned. Students modify partially completed programs by typing in code at their workstations and then viewing the result. They can compare their results with that shown in the screen shots to ensure that their code is correct. In addition, when students are to read a file, they are shown how to use Notepad to examine a data file and its contents quickly—without the tedium of having to enter code; students can also use Notepad to make modifications to the data files.

- Tips: These notes provide additional information and professional "best practices." For example, students might be cautioned to avoid a common error, given a rule of thumb, or told the outcome of changing a variable.

- Chapter summaries: Following each chapter is a summary that recaps the programming concepts and techniques covered in the chapter. This feature provides a concise means for students to review and check their understanding of the main points in each chapter.

- Review Questions: Questions at the end of the chapters reinforce main ideas introduced. Successfully answering these questions will demonstrate mastery of the concepts and information presented.

- Exercises: Each chapter concludes with exercises taken from *Programming Logic and Design*. These exercises provide students with additional practice of the skills and concepts they learned in the chapter.

ACKNOWLEDGMENTS

I would like to thank all of the people who helped to make this book a reality, especially DeVona Dors, Development Editor, whose support, hard work, and attention to detail have made this a quality textbook. Thank you, DeVona, for making my job easier and for all your encouragement. Thanks also to Tricia Boyle, Senior Product Manager; Pamela Elizian, Production Editor; and Nicole Ashton, Manuscript Quality Assurance Technical Lead. It has been a privilege to work with so many fine people who are dedicated to producing quality instructional materials.

I am grateful to the many reviewers who provided helpful and insightful comments during the development of this book, including R. Scott Cost, University of Maryland—Baltimore County; Anne Nelson, High Point University; Pam Silvers, Asheville-Buncombe Technical Community College; and especially Volker Gaul, Mid-state Technical College, whose recommendations were invaluable. I would also like to thank Tina Ostrander (Highline Community College), our Technical Editor, who did a great deal toward helping us produce a clean, error-free book.

Thanks also to Jim Scherbak, Bryant & Stratton College, Willoughby Hills Campus; and to Bruce Coscia, Bryant & Stratton College, Cleveland Downtown Campus. They provided resources, advice, and schedule adjustments so that I could complete this task. I appreciate all they did.

And finally, thanks to my wife, JoAnn, for her patience, sympathy, and faith throughout the writing process. In countless little ways, from reading a paragraph to reminding me that I was competent, she made a large contribution. This book is dedicated to her and to my son and daughter, Daniel and Angela.

Donald Vicarel

■ ■ ■ ■ READ THIS BEFORE YOU BEGIN

TO THE USER

STUDENT FILES

To complete the practice activities and exercises in this textbook, you will need the student files, which consist of partially completed programs that you are to modify and finish. Your instructor will provide you with the student files. You also can obtain them electronically from the Course Technology Web site by connecting to **http://www.course.com**, and then searching for this textbook's title.

SOLUTIONS

Solutions to review questions, practice activities, and exercises are provided to instructors on the Course Technology Web site at **www.course.com**. The solutions are password protected.

USING YOUR OWN COMPUTER

To use your own computer to complete the material in this textbook, you will need the following:

- A 486-level or higher personal computer running Microsoft Windows. This book was quality-assurance tested using Microsoft Windows XP.
- Microsoft Visual Studio .NET 2003 Professional Edition or Enterprise Edition, or Microsoft Visual Basic .NET 2003 Standard Edition.

VISIT OUR WORLD WIDE WEB SITE

Additional materials designed especially for you might be available for your course on the World Wide Web. Go to **http://www.course.com**. Periodically search this site for more details.

TO THE INSTRUCTOR

To complete the practice activities and exercises in this book, your students must use a set of student files. These files are available on the Course Technology Web site at **http://www.course.com**. Follow the instructions in the Help file to download the files to your server or stand-alone computer. You can view the Help file using a text editor such as WordPad or Notepad. Once the files are downloaded, you may instruct your students how to copy the files to their own computers or workstations.

Each practice activity or exercise in this textbook has a partially completed program for the student to finish. Because Visual Basic .NET programs (Microsoft refers to them as "solutions") are made up of several files, each practice activity or exercise has a folder of its own, and the folder's name is the title used in the activity or exercise. In addition, most of the activities and exercises in this textbook also make use of sequential (text) files consisting of data that must be processed. The data file for each solution is in the same folder as the solution's other files. Thus, a single folder contains all the material needed to complete one activity or exercise. The folders are grouped by chapter, and there are nine chapter folders that comprise the set of student files.

COURSE TECHNOLOGY STUDENT FILES

You are granted a license to copy the student files to any computer or computer network used by individuals who have purchased this book.

GETTING STARTED

In this chapter, you will learn how to do the following:

- ☐ Identify the major features of Visual Studio .NET
- ☐ Identify the components of a Visual Basic .NET solution
- ☐ Distinguish between object-oriented programming and procedural programming
- ☐ Start Visual Basic .NET, run a solution, and exit the solution
- ☐ Distinguish between design time and run time in Visual Basic .NET

Microsoft Visual Studio .NET is a programming environment made up of several different languages, one of which is **Visual Basic .NET** (referred to here as VB .NET). You will begin by examining this environment. Next, you will study the components of a program to see what it looks like when a programmer works on it and when a user runs it.

This textbook is intended to be a companion to Joyce Farrell's textbook, *Programming Logic and Design, Third Edition* (Boston: Course Technology, 2004). Throughout this textbook, you will see many references to Farrell's textbook (hereafter referred to as the *Logic* textbook or as *Logic*). To complete this chapter, you should have already read the first four chapters of *Logic*.

THE VISUAL STUDIO .NET IDE

VB .NET is one of the languages in a much larger integrated software development environment called Microsoft Visual Studio .NET. This environment is often referred to as an **integrated development environment (IDE)** because it includes not only the programming languages but also all the tools needed to build forms and to test and debug software applications. In addition, Visual Studio .NET allows certain programming languages to share the same tools and resources and permits blocks of code (called **procedures**) created in different languages to be used in the same program (called a **solution**). In other words, Visual Studio .NET allows you to create part of a solution in Visual Basic and then import other parts written in certain other languages. You won't be doing any of that in this textbook, however. Instead, you will use a limited number of VB .NET features to explore the programming concepts presented in *Logic*.

Although Visual Studio .NET is completely customizable, this book assumes you are using its **default** settings, that is, the settings are unchanged from when they were originally set. If you share your computer with other Visual Studio .NET programmers, your screens may appear different from the ones shown in this textbook. If so, see your instructor or system administrator for assistance.

To examine the Visual Studio .NET IDE, work through the following steps:

1. Click **Start** on the taskbar.
2. Move the pointer to **Programs** (or **All Programs**, depending on which version of Windows you are using). A list of programs and folders will appear.
3. Move the pointer to the **Microsoft Visual Studio .NET 2003** folder. A list of three items will appear.
4. Click the file **Microsoft Visual Studio .NET 2003**. A "splash screen" showing the languages and other products installed with your version of Visual Studio .NET will briefly appear (Figure 1-1), and then the IDE will open (Figure 1-2).

FIGURE 1-1: THE VISUAL STUDIO .NET SPLASH SCREEN

Installed Products from the Visual Studio Family:

Microsoft Visual Basic .NET   Microsoft Visual C# .NET   Microsoft Visual J# .NET   Microsoft Visual C++ .NET   Crystal Reports

FIGURE 1-2: THE VISUAL STUDIO .NET IDE WITH START PAGE WINDOW

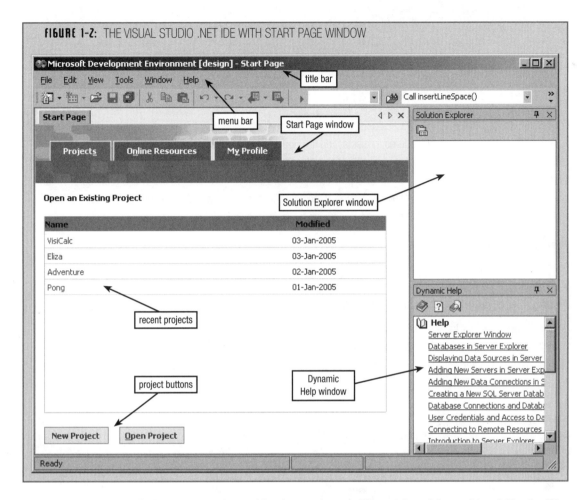

5. Verify that your screen resembles the one shown in Figure 1-2, and then quit by clicking the **File** menu, and then clicking **Exit**.

Starting and exiting is simple enough, but Figure 1-2 deserves further scrutiny. The IDE shown in Figure 1-2 contains three windows—the Start Page window and two Tool Windows (Solution Explorer and Dynamic Help).

At the top of the IDE is the title bar. Immediately beneath it is the menu bar, showing six menus: File, Edit, View, Tools, Window, and Help. Each menu contains its own list of commands. The menu bar is **dynamic**, that is, the menus and their commands will change when you work on different tasks.

TIP □ □ □ □   In addition to selecting commands from menus, many commands can also be selected by clicking icons, which appear in toolbars, or by using "shortcut keys." For consistency's sake, this textbook uses menus for most commands, but as you gain experience, you will probably find quicker and more efficient ways.

Beneath the menu bar is the the Start Page window. The **Start Page** allows you to open an existing project, create a new one, or customize the IDE. This window will be replaced by others when you open and work on a project. To the right of the screen are the Solution Explorer and Dynamic Help windows. **Solution Explorer** displays the components of a solution while you are working on it. This window is presently empty. **Dynamic Help** provides links to context-sensitive "help" files and is similar to the help provided in other Windows applications.

EXAMINING THE COMPONENTS OF A VB .NET SOLUTION

As you work through the practice activities and exercises in this textbook, you may think of your creations as "programs," but VB .NET refers to them as procedures, projects, and solutions. Roughly speaking, a **procedure** is a block of code that accomplishes a specific task, a **project** is a collection of procedures, and a **solution** is a collection of projects. However, the solutions in this textbook consist of only one project, and several of those projects have only one procedure. Therefore, this textbook employs the term "solution" in the same sense as "program," which is defined in Chapter 1 of *Logic*, and it employs the term "procedure" in the same sense as "module," which is defined in Chapter 4 of *Logic*.

THE SOLUTION FOLDER

The first solution you will examine is called **Doubler**, which was discussed in Chapter 1 of the *Logic* textbook. The solution implements the flowchart in *Logic*, Figure 1-7. When the user inputs a number, the solution doubles it and displays the result. Before opening the solution, you will examine Doubler as it is stored on disk.

Open the **Doubler** folder located in the **ch01** folder in your student files. It opens to reveal the files shown in Figure 1-3. (If, instead of the filenames as shown in the figure, you see extensions on *all* the filenames, you can go to the **Folder Options** in Windows and select **Hide extensions for known File types**). Note especially the icons that represents the Doubler solution and the Doubler project.

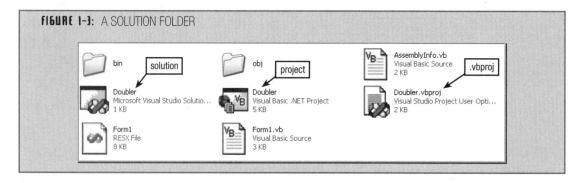

FIGURE 1-3: A SOLUTION FOLDER

The Doubler folder holds eight items—six files and two folders, which, in turn, contain even more files. Despite these eight items, the solution contains only one project, which, in turn, contains only one procedure. Next, you will examine the Doubler solution.

THE DESIGNER WINDOW

A programmer working on a VB .NET solution uses two windows. The Designer window is used for designing forms. The Code window is used for entering the code statements that make up the program, or solution. Work through the following steps to open the Doubler solution and examine its Designer window:

1. Refer to Figure 1-3 and double-click either the **Doubler** solution or the **Doubler** project (but not the file titled Doubler.vbproj). The solution will open in VB .NET.

2. Compare your screen with that shown in Figure 1-4. The Designer window, the white area shown in the figure, is not yet visible on your screen. Instead, your window is completely gray. Move your mouse pointer to the **Solution Explorer** window, and then click **Form1.vb**. Next, click the **View** menu, and then click **Designer**. The Designer window should now be visible on your screen, and inside it you should see the Doubler form as shown in Figure 1-4.

3. Figure 1-4 shows the Toolbox to the left of the Designer window. If you don't see it on your screen, click the **View** menu, then click **Toolbox**. The **pushpin** at the top of the toolbox should be pointing downward. If it isn't, click it.

4. Your screen should now look like that shown in Figure 1-4.

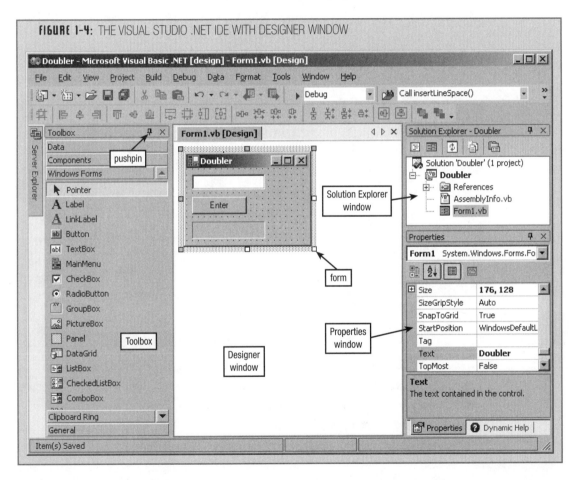

FIGURE 1-4: THE VISUAL STUDIO .NET IDE WITH DESIGNER WINDOW

Form1.vb shown in the Designer window in Figure 1-4 contains a white text box, a button that reads "Enter," and a gray label. These are discussed in Chapter 2. For now, merely notice that the Doubler form is covered with dots, called "grid points." Incidentally, also notice that the Solution Explorer window is no longer empty—it lists the files and folders that comprise the Doubler solution.

In the Designer window, a programmer designs a form by getting objects from the Toolbox and placing them on the form. These objects, also known as **controls**, give object-oriented programming its name. The *Logic* textbook, on the other hand, employs procedural-programming techniques. You can find a comparison of the two techniques in *Logic*, Chapter 1, under the heading "Understanding the Evolution of Programming Techniques." Because *Logic* takes the procedural approach, you won't spend much time in the Designer window as you work through this textbook. The two textbooks make their connection in the code window, where you will write VB .NET code statements that correspond to the pseudocode in the *Logic* textbook.

THE CODE WINDOW

In addition to working on a form, a programmer must also write code, so that the objects on the form actually *do* something when a user runs the solution. Switching from the Designer window to the Code window is simple and is described in the following steps:

1. Click the **View** menu, then click **Code**. The Code window shown in Figure 1-5 will appear.

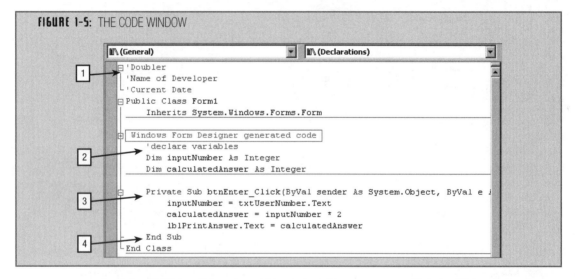

FIGURE 1-5: THE CODE WINDOW

2. Notice (1) the **heading** region, which consists of three comments, (2) the **variables declaration** region, (3) the **procedure header**, which begins **Private Sub btnEnter_Click** and (4) the **procedure footer**, which is **End Sub**. These areas will be of concern when you write your own code, and they will be discussed in later chapters.
3. Return to the form by clicking the **View** menu, and then clicking **Designer**.

DESIGN-TIME AND RUN-TIME OPERATING MODES

Visual Studio .NET has three modes of operation, two of which are relevant here. **Design time** (also called **design mode**) is for creating and modifying a solution. **Run time** (or **run mode**) is for testing a solution. The third, **break mode**, which is used for debugging longer solutions, will not be discussed in this textbook.

As you have seen, in design time you can work on either the form in the Designer window or the code in the Code window. When in run time, the solution is running. The form appears as a window on the screen, and you can interact with the solution as a user would.

STARTING AND STOPPING A SOLUTION

A user never sees a solution in the same way as you do. When a solution is "put into production" (as discussed in *Logic*, Chapter 1), it is made into an executable file, and a user sees nothing but the form(s) at run time. You, on the other hand, have two roles: You need not only to work on the form and the code in design time but also to play the role of user to test your solution. The following steps will allow you to see the form and interact with it in run time as a user would.

1. Regardless of whether you are in the Designer window or the Code window, click the **Debug** menu, and then click **Start**. After several moments of compiling, the run-time form will appear.

2. Notice that the grid points, which were visible at design time, are not present at run time. You can probably see the design-time version of the form in the background, but do not confuse it with the run-time version.

3. Notice that although the solution is in run time, nothing seems to be happening! The solution is indeed running, but it is waiting for an event to trigger a procedure. An **event** is an action that the computer recognizes, for example, the click of the mouse button. Because the procedures that make up Visual Basic .NET solutions must be triggered by events, VB .NET is referred to as an object-oriented, event-driven language. (This is another difference between object-oriented languages and procedural languages—the latter does not make use of events.)

4. In Doubler, the solution is waiting for you, the user, to click the Enter button. Type a number in the white text box, then click **Enter**. The number is doubled, and the result appears in the label at the bottom of the form. (See Figure 1-6.)

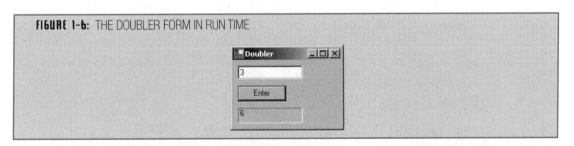

FIGURE 1-6: THE DOUBLER FORM IN RUN TIME

5. To stop the solution, click the **Debug** menu twice, then click **Stop Debugging**. The run-time form will disappear, and the solution will be back in design time.

6. To remove Doubler from the computer's memory, click the **File** menu, then click **Close Solution**. The Solution Explorer window will become empty again. At this point, you could open an existing solution or create a new one.

7. Close VB .NET by clicking the **File** menu, and then clicking **Exit**.

CHAPTER SUMMARY

This chapter provided a brief introduction to the Visual Studio .NET IDE and the Visual Basic .NET language. You examined and ran a solution that implemented a flowchart from Chapter 1 of *Programming Logic and Design*, and you navigated between design time and run time and between the Designer window and the Code window. The chapter presented these key points:

☐ Microsoft Visual Studio .NET is an integrated development environment (IDE) comprised of several languages and the additional tools needed to create software applications.

☐ Procedures are blocks of code that accomplish specific tasks. Projects are collections of procedures. A solution is a collection of projects.

☐ Visual Basic .NET is an object-oriented, event-driven language, in contrast to procedure-oriented languages.

☐ When a solution is in design time (also called design mode) it can be modified. When a solution is in run time (also called run mode), the program statements are executed by the computer, and the project cannot be modified until the solution's execution is stopped.

REVIEW QUESTIONS

Match each word or statement that follows with the definition or phrase that best describes it. Each item will be used only once.

1. _____ **default**

2. _____ **design time**

3. _____ **objects**

4. _____ **Designer window**

5. _____ **event**

6. _____ **form**

7. _____ **solution**

8. _____ **Solution Explorer**

9. _____ **Stop Debugging**

10. _____ **procedure**

a. the menu item to select to end run time and return to design time

b. a value that is initially set by the computer

c. the mode of operation during which a solution can be modified

d. text boxes, buttons, and labels that are placed on forms

e. an action that the computer recognizes

f. the place where a form is displayed during design time

g. a gray, rectangular area that the user perceives as a window when a solution is running

h. another name for "program"

i. a block of code that accomplishes a specific task

j. the window that lists all the files that comprise a solution

2 MODIFYING A SOLUTION

In this chapter, you will learn how to do the following:

- ☐ Copy a solution
- ☐ Identify and describe the purpose of remarks, line spaces, variable declarations, and procedure headers and footers
- ☐ Modify existing code
- ☐ Identify and correct a logic error
- ☐ Describe three common data types used in VB .NET
- ☐ Print a form and the code for a solution

In Chapter 1, you ran a Visual Basic .NET solution called **Doubler**. In Chapter 2, you will modify an existing solution in several ways. The activities will acquaint you with some of the terminology of VB .NET. To complete this chapter, you should have read the first four chapters of Joyce Farrell's textbook, *Programming Logic and Design, Third Edition*.

DUPLICATING A FOLDER

In Chapter 1, you discovered that a solution consists of many files stored in the same folder. Modifying a solution in VB .NET, therefore, is not as simple as in other software applications. For instance, in Word you can modify a document and use a simple *Save As* command to save the revised version with a different name. In the case of VB .NET, however, you will need first to make a copy of the original folder and its contents, and then make your modifications to the *copy*. In this way, the original folder will always remain intact, and you can always return to it if necessary. Before beginning this chapter's practice activities, you will need to duplicate a folder. Use the following steps:

1. Open the **ch02** folder in your student files.
2. If you know how to duplicate a folder on your own, copy **Inc Doubler Two**, and then paste it so *both* the original and the duplicate folders are inside folder **ch02**. If you need help, follow the instructions in **Appendix A**.
3. The duplicate folder is titled **Copy of Inc Doubler Two**. Change the name to **Doubler Two**.
4. Open the **Doubler Two** folder, and then double-click either the **Doubler Two** solution or the **Doubler Two** project (but *not* the file titled *Doubler Two.vbproj*). The solution will open in VB .NET. Your Solution Explorer window should list the same files as those shown in Figure 2-1.

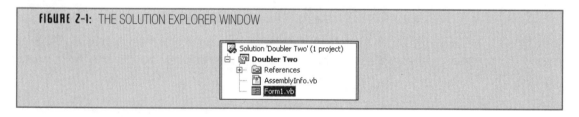

FIGURE 2-1: THE SOLUTION EXPLORER WINDOW

TESTING THE SOLUTION

It's always a good idea to test a solution frequently as you work on it. So, even before you begin your modifications, follow these steps:

1. Click the **Debug** menu, and then click **Start**. After a few moments, the form will appear in run time. It looks quite similar to the solution you ran in Chapter 1.
2. Type the number **2** in the text box at the top of the form, and then click the **Enter** button. The number **4** will appear on the label at the bottom of the form. The solution is supposed to double the number. So far, so good.

3. Type **3** in the text box at the top of the form, and then click the **Enter** button. The number **5** will appear. Oops! Three times two equals six, not five.

4. To stop executing the solution, click the **Debug** menu twice, and then click **Stop Debugging**.

You have a **bug**, or programming error. Chapter 1 of the *Logic* textbook discusses two kinds of programming errors. **Syntax errors** are language violations that prevent a program from compiling and executing. For example, if you substitute a slash (/) for one of the equals signs (=) in the code, when you click Debug|Start to run the solution, you will receive the message, "There were build errors."

On the other hand, **logic errors** do not stop a program from running. Logic errors do, however, yield incorrect results. Of the two types of bugs, logic errors are the more difficult to identify. Thus, Doubler Two, which has a logic error, runs— but it doesn't give you the correct results. Let's begin troubleshooting by examining the code.

OPENING THE CODE WINDOW

Before attempting to open the Code window, notice Figure 2-1 again. The figure shows that Form1.vb has been selected. If it is not selected, you will not be able to see the Code and the Designer options in the View menu.

1. If necessary, select Form1.vb by moving your pointer to the **Solution Explorer** window and then clicking **Form1.vb**.

2. Click the **View** menu, then click **Code**. The Code window will open as shown in Table 2-1.

TABLE 2-1: THE DOUBLER TWO CODE WINDOW

```
1  'Doubler Two
2  'Your Name
3  'Date
4  Public Class Form1
5      Inherits System.Windows.Forms.Form
6
7  Windows Form Designer generated code
8      'declare variables here
9      Dim intInputNumber As Integer
10     Dim intCalculatedAnswer As Integer
11
12     Private Sub btnEnter_Click(ByVal sender As Object...
13
14         'assign value from form
15         intInputNumber = txtUserNumber.Text
16
17         'perform calculations
18         intCalculatedAnswer = intInputNumber + 2
19
20         'display results
21         lblDisplayAnswer.Text = intCalculatedAnswer
22
23     End Sub
24 End Class
```

EXAMINING THE CODE

Your Code window should resemble the one shown in Table 2-1, except for the line numbers, which have been added to the table for reference purposes. The font colors you see on your screen (which are absent in the table) can be ignored. However, you might note that black is for text; green is for remarks, which will be discussed next; and blue is for reserved words. **Reserved words**, often referred to as **keywords**, are words that have a special meaning in VB .NET; therefore, they cannot be used to name variables, objects, or any of the other things a programmer needs to name. Let's look at some specific lines of code.

INTERNAL DOCUMENTATION

Notice that lines 1, 2, 3, 8, 14, 17, and 20 of the code in Table 2-1 all begin with an apostrophe ('), indicating that the lines are **remarks**, or comments. As Chapter 3 of *Logic* points out, remarks are "non-executing statements" that comprise "internal program documentation."

Lines 6, 11, 13, 16, 19, and 22 are blank lines, also known as **line spaces**. Line spaces, like remarks, are not executed and therefore can be used to enhance the readability of the code.

VARIABLE DECLARATION

Before a variable can be used, it must be **declared** by using the keyword `Dim` to give it a name and indicate its data type (lines 9 and 10 in Table 2-1). For the practice activities and end-of-chapter exercises in this textbook, variables will always be declared immediately beneath the words `Windows Form Designer generated code` (line 7 in Table 2-1).

Notice the names of the variables used in this solution. The first three letters of the variable names (int) indicate their data type (integer). This naming convention has been widely adopted by VB .NET programmers and is used throughout this textbook. However, for code that relates directly to the pseudocode in the *Logic* textbook, the variable names employed in the *Logic* textbook are used.

THE PROCEDURE HEADER AND FOOTER

Line 12 of the code in Table 2-1 begins with the words `Private Sub` and is the procedure header. Line 23 consists of the words `End Sub` and is the procedure footer. Between the header and footer are the lines of code which make up the procedure itself. A well-written procedure contains the code to accomplish a single, specific task.

TIP ▫ ▫ ▫ ▫ | Chapter 3 in the *Logic* textbook discusses breaking down complex programming tasks into manageable modules. In Visual Basic, this modularization is accomplished through procedures. Although an ill-written procedure can become the "spaghetti" mentioned in *Logic*, Visual Basic was created with modularization in mind—unlike older languages such as COBOL and the early versions of BASIC.

MODIFYING THE CODE

Next, we'll correct the solution's logic error. VB .NET's code editor works just like a word processor, so you should not experience difficulty in the practice activities that follow. Be careful, though: If you delete the wrong segments of code, the solution will no longer run.

CHANGE THE HEADING

Whether you are in the workplace or in the classroom, when you modify a solution, you should always take time to modify the documentation. Use the following steps to change the heading of the Doubler Two solution.

1. Change line 2 so that it shows your own name. Keep the apostrophe.
2. Change line 3 to show the current date. Keep the apostrophe.

UNDERSTAND THE CODE

Figure 2-2 shows the movement of data between the form and the variables. The variable, `intInputNumber` gets its value from the text box `txtUserNumber`. The label `lblDisplayAnswer` gets its value from the variable `intCalculatedAnswer`.

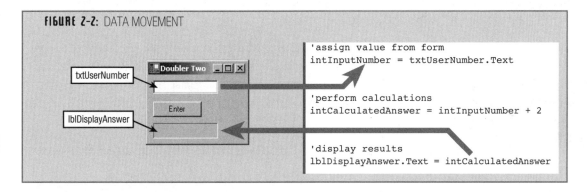

FIGURE 2-2: DATA MOVEMENT

```
'assign value from form
intInputNumber = txtUserNumber.Text

'perform calculations
intCalculatedAnswer = intInputNumber + 2

'display results
lblDisplayAnswer.Text = intCalculatedAnswer
```

CORRECT THE LOGIC ERROR

When you ran the solution, you entered a 3 into the text box. The procedure copied the 3 to the variable `intInputNumber`. (See Figure 2-2.) Next, the procedure calculated (or *mis*calculated) 3 + 2 and placed the sum, 5, in the variable `intCalculatedAnswer`. Finally, the procedure copied the 5 in `intCalculatedAnswer` to the label. To correct the error, simply change the addition sign to a multiplication sign, as indicated in the following steps.

1. Replace the addition sign (**+**) with the multiplication sign (*****). When you are finished, *do not press the* **Enter** *key*. Instead, merely click somewhere else in the Code window.
2. Verify that you have done everything correctly by running the solution: Click the **Debug** menu, and then click **Start**. During the time between your click of the Start button and the appearance of the run-time form, the VB .NET editor saves any changes you have made to the solution. In other words, any modifications you make to a solution are automatically saved every time you run the solution.

3. Type a **3** in the text box at the top of the form, and then click the **Enter** button. The number 6 should appear in the label. It appears that the bug is fixed.

4. Next, type **1.2** in the text box, and click the **Enter** button. The number 2.4 should appear in the label, but instead you see a 2. Oops! Another logic error—the procedure is not supposed to be dropping the decimal part of the number.

5. Try another number: Enter a **2.9**. A 6 is displayed!

6. Stop the procedure by clicking **Debug** twice, and then clicking **Stop Debugging**. Next, we'll look at how to identify and correct this problem.

CHANGING DATA TYPES

Another reason that logic errors are more difficult to spot than syntax errors is that sometimes they show up only when certain types of data are involved: In this case, as long as you enter whole numbers, everything works fine—the error is not raised, or evident, until you enter a number with a decimal fraction. The problem with the procedure is not that the decimal part of the number gets dropped, but that it gets rounded. Your 1.2 was rounded to 1, and when doubled, $1 \times 2 = 2$; similarly, your 2.9 was rounded to 3, and when doubled, $3 \times 2 = 6$. The source of the problem can be seen in Table 2-1, lines 9 and 10. The problem is that the variables were declared as integers.

Chapter 1 of the *Logic* textbook acknowledges two basic data types, *character* and *numeric*, and then subdivides numeric data types into *integer* and *floating-point.* This textbook will employ the same three data types, but VB . NET requires that the data types be declared as **String** (for text), **Integer** (for whole numbers), and **Decimal** (for floating-point numbers, including currency and fractions). VB .NET recognizes many more data types, but three will suffice for the practice activities and end-of-chapter exercises in this textbook.

The solution to the rounding problem is simply to declare the variables as decimals rather than integers. To do that, follow these steps:

1. Substitute the following two lines for lines 9 and 10:

```
Dim decInputNumber As Decimal
Dim decCalculatedAnswer As Decimal
```

2. In lines 15 and 18, change the variable name **intInputNumber** to **decInputNumber**.

3. In lines 18 and 21, change the variable name **intCalculatedAnswer** to **decCalculatedAnswer**.

4. Test the solution with a value of **1.2**. If the display reads 2.4, you have successfully "debugged" the procedure.

5. Do not stop the solution! In the next activity, you will print out the run-time form, and the solution must remain running. Leave it as it is, with the form displaying 1.2 in the text box and 2.4 in the label.

OBTAINING A HARDCOPY

Presumably you are working through this textbook as part of a credit course. If so, your instructor will undoubtedly require you to submit some evidence that you have successfully completed the practice activities and end-of-chapter exercises. Printing out the form and the code provides one form of evidence. Furthermore, your code printouts can help you to complete future practice activities and exercises.

1. Verify that you are in run time, that you typed **1.2** in the text box, and that **2.4** is displayed in the label.
2. To print out the form, follow the procedure described in **Appendix B**. Then return to this series of steps.
3. Stop executing the solution by clicking the **Debug** menu twice, and then clicking **Stop Debugging**.
4. To print out the code, verify that you are in design time and in the **Code** window, then click the **File** menu, and then click **Print**.

CHAPTER SUMMARY

This chapter provided you with some hands-on experience debugging a solution and modifying code. The following key points were presented:

- Remarks and line spaces are non-executing and are ignored when a solution in compiled. Their purpose is internal documentation—they make a solution easier to understand.

- Before a variable can be used, it must be declared by using a `Dim` statement to provide a name and a data type.

- Two of the most common types of error are: syntax errors and logic errors. Syntax errors occur when the code does not conform to the programming language rules. By contrast, logic errors allow the code to run, but they yield incorrect results. Logic errors are difficult to locate for two reasons: First, they don't stop a solution from running; second, they sometimes show up only when certain data are involved.

- The data types used in this textbook are String (text), Integer (whole number), and Decimal (currency and fractions).

- To print out a form, make sure you are in run time, then use Alt+PrintScreen to take a snapshot of the active window, paste it into a Word or a Wordpad document, and then print the document.

- To print out code, make sure you are in design time, and then click Print on the File menu.

REVIEW QUESTIONS

For each statement, select the term that best completes each sentence.

1. _____ **declares a variable for a person's pay rate in VB .NET.**
   a. `Dim curPayRate As Currency`
   b. `Dim decPayRate As Decimal`
   c. `Dim intPayRate As Integer`
   d. `Dim strPayRate As String`

2. **A remark** _____ **.**
   a. begins with an apostrophe
   b. is not executed when the solution runs
   c. is internal documentation
   d. All of the above are true.

3.   **A logic error** _____ .

    a. stops a solution from running, i.e., it causes a "break"

    b. is another name for syntax error

    c. is easy to spot

    d. may only show up when certain data are involved in the solution

4.   **To print a form** _____ .

    a. the solution should be in run time

    b. the solution should be in design time

    c. the solution should be in break time

    d. the solution can be in either run time or design time

5.   **In VB .NET, three common data types are called** _____ .

    a. String, Floating-point, and Currency

    b. Integer, Decimal, and Currency

    c. Decimal, Integer, and String

    d. Character, Decimal, and Floating-point

EXERCISE

Debug the Div2 solution:

1.   Your **ch02** folder contains a folder called **Inc Div2**. Duplicate the folder and rename it from **Copy of Inc Div2** to **Div2**.

2.   Open the **Div2** solution. The Div2 solution is supposed to accept a number that the user enters into the text box, divide that number by **2**, and then display the quotient in the label at the bottom of the form.

3.   The solution has a logic error and several syntax errors. Using your code from Doubler Two as a reference, debug Div2.

4.   Submit the run-time form and the code per your instructor's requirements.

3

READING A RECORD

In this chapter, you will learn how to do the following:

- ☐ Examine and determine the record structure of a sequential file
- ☐ Open a sequential file, read a record, and close the file
- ☐ Remove objects from a form
- ☐ Create a Form_Load event handler

In Chapter 2, values for variables were obtained from a user who entered information into a text box and then pressed an *Enter* button. The act of clicking a button is an **event**, and the procedure triggered by the event is referred to as an **event handler**, or an **event procedure**. In this chapter, procedures will input information from data files. You will use a `Form_Load` event to trigger the procedure. To prepare for this chapter, you should have read the first four chapters of Joyce Farrell's textbook, *Programming Logic and Design, Third Edition*.

EXAMINING A TEXT FILE IN NOTEPAD

When working with a data file, the more you know about it in advance, the easier your programming tasks will be. Therefore, if you can open data file, do so, and note the number of fields and their data types.

Visual Basic is frequently called upon to process data from databases and spreadsheets in which data is arranged in fields and records, as described in the *Logic* textbook, Chapter 1. The simplest kind of data files, known as **sequential files**, are merely text files that store data by using commas (,) and **carriage returns** (produced by pressing the Enter key) to organize data into separate fields and records. Because Notepad is an application that can create text files, it can be used to create, examine, and change sequential files (see Appendix E). In the following practice activity, you will use Notepad to examine two files.

1. Open the **Inc Plus100** folder located in the **ch03** folder in your student files.
2. Open the **bin** folder that is inside the **Inc Plus100** folder.
3. Double-click the **Five Primes** file. It will open in Notepad.
4. Observe that there are five data in the file, each on a separate line. The data are numerical; specifically, they are integers. Note that the first number is a 2.
5. Click the **File** menu, and then click **Exit**. Notepad and the file will close.
6. Exit the **bin** folder by clicking the **Back** button, as shown in Figure 3-1. This will return you to the **Inc Plus100** folder.

FIGURE 3-1: BACKING OUT OF THE BIN FOLDER

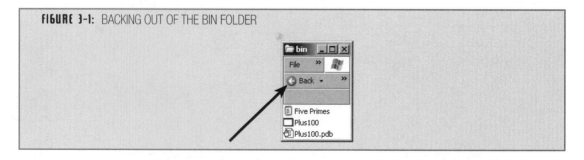

7. Click the **Back** button again to exit the **Inc Plus100** folder and return to the **ch03** folder.
8. In the **ch03** folder, open the **TwoNames Corrected** folder, and then open the **bin** folder that it contains.
9. Double-click the **Five Presidents** file. It will open in Notepad.

10. Notice that the file consists of the first and last names of five United States Presidents. In data-processing terms (see *Logic* Chapter 1), there are five records (the five presidents), made up of two fields each (the last name and the first name). Notice that the records are separated by carriage returns, and the fields are separated by commas.

11. Click the **File** menu, and then click **Exit**. Notepad and the file will close.

READING A SEQUENTIAL FILE

In Chapters 1 and 2, your solutions obtained their data from users who entered information into text boxes on forms. In the following practice activity, you will adapt one of those procedures to obtain data from a file, rather than from a form. You will begin by duplicating and renaming a partially completed solution:

1. Open the **ch03** folder in your student files.

2. If you know how to duplicate a folder on your own, copy **Inc Plus100**, and then paste it so both the original and the duplicate folders are inside folder **ch03**. If you need help, follow the instructions in **Appendix A**.

3. Rename the duplicate folder from **Copy of Inc Plus100** to **Plus100**.

4. Open the **Plus100** folder, and then double-click either the **Plus100** solution or the **Plus100** project. It will open in VB .NET.

When you open for the first time a solution you have duplicated, the document window (the large, central window on your screen) will appear gray, and the View menu will not display the Code and Designer options. To remedy this situation, simply select the solution's form by going to the Explorer window at the right side of your screen and clicking Form1.vb. When you have selected Form1.vb, you will be able to choose the Code and Designer options from the File menu.

UNDERSTANDING THE PLUS100 SOLUTION

Before modifying the Plus100 solution to input data from a sequential file, run the unmodified solution by working through the following steps:

1. Click the **Debug** menu, and then click **Start**.

2. Enter a **43** in the text box, and then click the **Enter** button. The label will display 143. The procedure, an event handler, is triggered by clicking the Enter button. It adds 100 to the number input by the user and then displays the result in the label on the form.

3. Stop the solution, click the **View** menu, and then click **Code**. (If you do not see the word, "Code" in the View menu, move your pointer to the **Solution Explorer** window and click **Form1.vb**. Then return to the **View** menu and click **Code**.)

4. Examine your code window, especially the `btnEnter_Click` procedure, which is shown in Table 3-1. Notice that you have three lines of actual code and two line spaces (blank lines). Note that the procedure header shown in line 1 cannot be seen in its entirety without scrolling to the right.

TABLE 3-1: THE PROCEDURE FOR THE PLUS100 SOLUTION

```
1 Private Sub btnEnter_Click(ByVal sender As System.Object, ByVal e...
2
3       intInputNumber = txtUserNumber.Text
4       intCalculatedAnswer = intInputNumber + 100
5
6       lblDisplayAnswer.Text = intCalculatedAnswer
7 End Sub
```

This solution does practically the same thing as the Doubler solution in Chapter 1 (Figure 1-6): The procedure is triggered when the user clicks the button named **btnEnter**. In line 3 of Table 3-1, the procedure takes the value in the text box and copies it to a variable called **intInputNumber**. In line 4, 100 is added to the number, and the result is assigned to a variable called **intCalculatedAnswer**. In line 6, the calculated answer is displayed as output in the label on the form.

MODIFYING THE PLUS100 SOLUTION

Obtaining data from a file involves three steps: opening the file, inputting information from the file, and then closing the file. In Table 3-1, the line space at line 2 is where you will enter the code that opens the file. Next, you will change line 3 so that it inputs a number from the file, rather than from the text box on the form. Finally, the line space at line 5 is where you will close the file. Table 3-2 shows the modified solution.

 **TIP**   Whenever you create a procedure that *outputs* information to a file, it is critical that you close the file at the conclusion of the output operation so all the data will be saved. This is not an issue when a procedure *inputs* information, as we are doing here; nevertheless, it is a good habit to close a file when you are through using it.

TABLE 3-2: THE MODIFIED PROCEDURE FOR THE PLUS100 SOLUTION

```
1 Private Sub btnEnter_Click(ByVal sender As System.Object, ByVal e...
2       FileOpen(1, "Five Primes.txt", OpenMode.Input)
3       Input(1, intInputNumber)
4       intCalculatedAnswer = intInputNumber + 100
5       FileClose(1)
6       lblDisplayAnswer.Text = intCalculatedAnswer
7 End Sub
```

Notice Table 3-2 line 2: **FileOpen** is the VB .NET statement that opens a file. It requires three items of information that must be enclosed in parentheses and separated by commas: The first is a file number, in this case, 1. The second is the path with filename and extension. A **path** indicates the nest of folders in which the file is stored (see Appendix C). However, because this textbook uses the default location (the solution's bin folder), only the filename and extension must be specified. The extension, **.txt** identifies the file as a text file. The last item of information that **FileOpen** requires is the **OpenMode**, which specifies whether you intend to access the file for input, output, or for some other type of access. For reading from a file, the **OpenMode**. is *Input*. Incidentally, when referring to a file in your code, you will always use its file *number*, and never its *filename*.

TIP ◻ ◻ ◻ ◻ | VB .NET can accommodate solutions with 255 files open simultaneously, as long as each has its own unique file number, which can be any integer from 1 to 255.

Line 3 in Table 3-2 shows the **Input** statement, which reads a piece of data from file number 1 and assigns it to the variable, `intInputNumber`. Unlike the `FileOpen` statement, the `Input` statement requires only two pieces of information: a file number and a variable name.

Line 5 in Table 3-2 shows the **FileClose** statement, which closes the file having the number that is in parentheses after the statement. The file number is optional, and if it is omitted, `FileClose` will close any and all files that are open.

The following practice activity will walk you through the steps to modify the Plus100 solution:

1. Enter the statement to open the **Five Primes** file, as shown in Table 3-2, line 2. Make sure you include all the punctuation shown.
2. In line 3, replace the words **intInputNumber = txtUserNumber.Text** with the words **Input (1, intInputNumber)**
3. In line 5, enter **FileClose(1)**

Because your solution will now be obtaining its data from a file rather than a text box, you no longer need the text box, so you can remove it from the form. Continue to work through the following steps to delete the text box:

1. Click the **View** menu, and then click **Designer**.
2. Click the text box at the top of the form. **Resize handles** (eight tiny squares around the periphery of the text box) will appear to show that it has been selected (Figure 3-2).

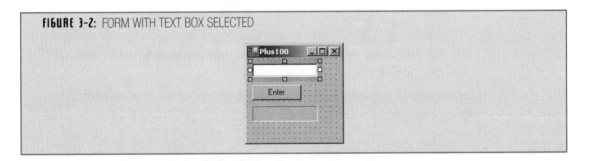

FIGURE 3-2: FORM WITH TEXT BOX SELECTED

3. Press the **Delete** key on the keyboard. The text box will disappear.
4. Open the Code window by clicking the **View** menu, and then clicking **Code**.
5. Change the heading comments as follows:
   a. Change the title in the first remark from **Plus100** to **Plus100 with File Input**.
   b. Place your name or initials and the date in the next two remarks.
6. Click the **Debug** menu, and then click **Start**. Your modified Plus100 solution will automatically be saved, and after a few moments the run-time form will appear, but nothing will happen: Although

you no longer need to type a number as you did in the previous version, you still need to click the **Enter** button to trigger the procedure.

7. Click the **Enter** button. After a moment or so, the number 102 will appear in the label. Recall that 2 was the first number in the Five Primes file; consequently, the number displayed in the label is 2 plus 100, or 102.

8. To stop the solution click **Debug**, and then click **Stop Debugging**.

You may recall that the Five Primes file contains five numbers. What happened to the other four? Your solution used the input statement only once then closed the file immediately thereafter, so only one number was read and displayed. In the next chapter, you will learn how to process a whole file.

A FORM_LOAD EVENT HANDLER

When you ran the previous solution, you may have noticed that once the solution was started, there was nothing for the user to do but click the Enter button. The solution does not need to interact with the user to complete its tasks. Many data-processing applications work in the same manner. In fact, none of the file-reading programs in the *Logic* textbook or the remaining solutions in this textbook are interactive.

Therefore, you can delete the Enter button just as you deleted the text box. However, you will still need some event to trigger the procedure. In the following practice activity, you will create a **Form_Load event handler**, that is, a procedure that executes as soon as the form is called into memory.

1. Return to the **Designer** window, so you can see your form.

2. Select the **Enter** button by clicking it one time. When the resize handles appear around it, press the **Delete** key on the keyboard. The button will disappear from the form.

3. Double-click the form. (Make sure you double-click the form itself and not the label that is on the form.) The code window will open and a procedure header (**Private Sub Form1_Load...**) and footer (**End Sub**) will appear.

4. Cut the five lines of code which are in the **btnEnter_Click** procedure and paste them in the **Form1_Load** procedure, as diagrammed in Figure 3-3.

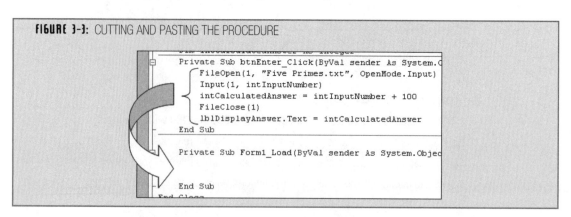

FIGURE 3-3: CUTTING AND PASTING THE PROCEDURE

```
      Dim intCalculatedAnswer As Integer
□     Private Sub btnEnter_Click(ByVal sender As System.O
        FileOpen(1, "Five Primes.txt", OpenMode.Input)
        Input(1, intInputNumber)
        intCalculatedAnswer = intInputNumber + 100
        FileClose(1)
        lblDisplayAnswer.Text = intCalculatedAnswer
      End Sub

      Private Sub Form1_Load(ByVal sender As System.Objec


      End Sub
    End Class
```

5. Since the **btnEnter_Click** event handler is now an empty procedure, you can delete the header and footer. Incidentally, the complete header is:

```
Private Sub btnEnter_Click(ByVal sender As System.Object,
ByVal e As System.EventArgs)
```

If you want to view the whole line, you will have to scroll to the right. The footer is the simple **End Sub**. You can delete the header and footer in the same way as you delete text using a word processor.

6. Click **Debug**, and then click **Start**. The solution will run by itself.

7. To stop, click **Debug**, and then click **Stop Debugging**.

8. Exit VB .NET.

INPUTTING A WHOLE RECORD

A sequential file does not permit the selective reading of data. For example, a solution can't skip over the last names and just read the first names; rather, it must read through every item sequentially. Therefore, when working with a sequential file, you should input a whole record at a time—failing to do so will almost always produce logic errors. By way of illustration, consider the Five Presidents file that you examined earlier in this chapter. Its data is shown in Table 3-3.

TABLE 3-3: THE FIVE PRESIDENTS FILE

Washington,	George
Adams,	John
Jefferson,	Thomas
Madison,	James
Monroe,	James

Notice that the Five Presidents file contains 10 pieces of data, 5 records of 2 fields each. Suppose that a programmer wants to display just the first names of the first two presidents and works up the pseudocode that follows to solve the problem. The solution looks promising, but it doesn't accomplish the task:

```
Get FirstName
Display FirstName
Get FirstName
Display FirstName
```

It appears as if the solution will get the first name, then display it, then get the next first name, and then display it, too. However, the actual output is "Washington" and then "George". The solution reads the first piece of data, "Washington," assigns it to the **FirstName** variable, and then displays it. Next it reads the second piece of data, "George," assigns "George" to the **FirstName** variable, and then displays it. To see this solution in action and to view the actual Visual Basic code, you can open the **TwoNames With Errors** folder in the **ch03** folder in your student files, and then double-click either the **TwoNames** solution or the **TwoNames** project.

The correct solution reads a whole record at a time, as shown in the following pseudocode:

```
Get LastName
Get FirstName
Display FirstName
Get LastName
Get FirstName
Display FirstName
```

In this example, the solution reads "Washington" and assigns it to `LastName`, then reads "George" and assigns it to `FirstName`, and then displays `FirstName (George)`. Next, the solution reads "Adams" and assigns it to `LastName`, then reads "John" and assigns it to `FirstName`, and then displays `FirstName (John)`. To see this solution in action and to view the actual Visual Basic code, you can open the **TwoNames Corrected** folder in the **ch03** folder in your student files, and then double-click either the **TwoNames** solution or the **TwoNames** project.

UNDERSTANDING THE TWONAMES SOLUTION

Table 3-4 shows the code that comprises the TwoNames Corrected solution. The line numbers are not part of the solution but have been added for reference purposes.

TABLE 3-4: THE TWONAMES CORRECTED SOLUTION

```
1  'TwoNames Corrected
2  'L. Rudolph
3  'Nov 19, 1831
4  Public Class Form1
5      Inherits System.Windows.Forms.Form
6
7  Windows Form Designer generated code
8      'declare variables
9      Dim strFirstName As String
10     Dim strLastName As String
11
12     Private Sub Form1_Load(ByVal sender As System.Object, ByVal e...
13
14         FileOpen(1, "Five Presidents.txt", OpenMode.Input)
15
16         Input(1, strLastName)
17         Input(1, strFirstName)
18         lblFirstDisplay.Text = strFirstName
19
20         Input(1, strLastName)
21         Input(1, strFirstName)
22         lblSecondDisplay.text = strFirstName
23
24         FileClose(1)
25     End Sub
26 End Class
```

Notice the following details about the code shown in Table 3-4:

- Lines 1 through 3 show the solution heading, which includes the title, the programmer's name, and the date.
- The remark at line 8 is the beginning of the *variables declaration* region.
- Lines 9 and 10 show two variables are declared using the `Dim` statement; both are strings.
- Line 12 shows the procedure is a `Form_Load` event handler.
- Line 14 opens the file. The file number is `1` and the filename is `Five Presidents.txt`.
- Lines 16 and 17 read the first record. Notice that Input uses the file number (`1`) and not the filename (`Five Presidents`).
- Line 18 displays the first name field (in the variable `strFirstName`) from the first record.
- Lines 20 and 21 read the second record.
- Line 22 displays the first name field from the second record.
- Line 24 closes the file.

CHAPTER SUMMARY

In this chapter, you began working with sequential files. Most of the subsequent work in this textbook will involve reading sequential files and processing the data they contain. The following key points were presented:

❑ A sequential file is a text file that uses commas and carriage returns to separate fields and records.

❑ Notepad can be used to create, change, and examine sequential access files.

❑ Inputting information from a file involves three steps: opening the file, reading the data into variables, and closing the file.

❑ When reading a sequential file, a solution cannot skip over pieces of data to select what is needed, but it must read the data in sequence.

❑ A Form_Load event handler is a procedure that executes as soon as the form is called into memory.

REVIEW QUESTIONS

1. **Use the code shown in Table 3-5 to answer the questions that follow it. Assume that the programmer used the techniques and observed the conventions presented in this textbook.**

TABLE 3-5: A CODE EXAMPLE

```
1  'H. S. Truman
2  'T. E. Dewey
3  '26 dec 1972
4  Public Class Form1
5      Inherits System.Windows.Forms.Form
6
7  Windows Form Designer generated code
8      Dim strEvent As String
9      Dim intYear As Integer
10
11     Private Sub btnOnly_Click (ByVal sender As System.Object, By...
12         FileOpen(1, "Truman Biography.txt", OpenMode.Input)
13         Input(1, strEvent)
14         Input(1, intYear)
15         FileClose(1)
16         lblEventName.Text = strFirstName
17         lblDate.Text = intYear
18     End Sub
19 End Class
```

a. Who wrote the solution?
b. How many variables are declared?
c. What is/are the variable data type(s)?
d. What is the name of the file used in the solution?

e. Can you tell how many fields are in the file by examining the code in the table? If so, how many fields are there for each record?

f. Can you tell how many records are in the file by examining the code in the table? If so, how many records are there in the file?

g. Which lines read data contained in the file?

h. Which lines display information?

i. What event triggers the procedure?

2. **Open the CAMPERS file that is in the ch03 folder in your student files. Refer to CAMPERS to answer the following questions:**

a. How many records does CAMPERS have?

b. How many fields does it have?

c. Name the data type for each field

d. What value is shown in the fourth field of the second record?

e. What data type is shown in the second field of the fourth record?

4

READING A FILE

In this chapter, you will learn how to do the following:

- [ ] Relate procedure comments to flowchart shapes and pseudocode
- [ ] Describe how the EOF function is used in Visual Basic to control a loop
- [ ] Use a WHILE loop to read all the records in a sequential file
- [ ] Describe the elements of the Properties window
- [ ] Use the Properties window to set text and name properties
- [ ] Code a procedure to end a solution

In Chapter 3, your program solutions read the first record in a file and then stopped. In this chapter, your solution will read a whole file. In addition, you will begin to learn about the properties of the objects that are used in a solution. To prepare for this chapter, you should have read the first four chapters of Joyce Farrell's textbook, *Programming Logic and Design, Third Edition.*

A DATA-PROCESSING PARADIGM

Chapter 4 of the *Logic* textbook discusses a basic data-processing paradigm that is broken down into three modules. (See *Logic*, Figure 4-6: FLOWCHART AND PSEUDOCODE OF MAINLINE LOGIC.) It is very much like the following flowchart:

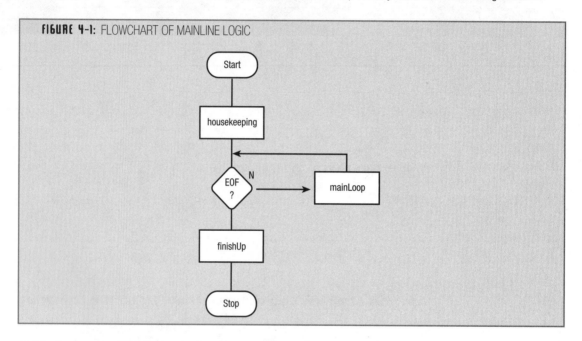

FIGURE 4-1: FLOWCHART OF MAINLINE LOGIC

In this chapter, you will implement the flowchart logic by displaying a list of the clothing items from the INVENTORY file that is presented in Chapter 4 of the *Logic* textbook. Although the *Logic* textbook enumerates several tasks to be accomplished in a housekeeping module, the housekeeping routine in your solution will do nothing more than open the INVENTORY file. Your main loop will consist of two tasks: First, it will read a record from the file. Second, it will output one of the fields, the item name, by adding it to a list displayed on the form. The EOF (end-of-file) decision shown in the flowchart indicates that this main loop is to be repeated until the end of the file has been reached. The finishUp routine merely closes the file you opened in the housekeeping routine.

EXAMINING THE INVENTORY FILE

The sequential file that you examined in the previous chapter used commas to separate the fields and carriage returns to separate the records. This made it easy for humans to discern the data. However, you should note that in sequential files, commas and carriage returns serve the same purpose (to separate the data) and can be used interchangeably.

As *Logic*, Chapter 4, Figure 4-9 illustrates, data "chunks" can be stored as a single, long stream of text. The INVENTORY file that you will examine next is such a stream, with only commas to **delimit** (separate) the data items. To discover where the records begin and end, you will need to look for a repeating pattern of data types as you work through the following activity.

1. Open the **Inc Inventory Reader** folder located in the **ch04** folder in your student files.
2. Open the **bin** folder that is inside the **Inc Inventory Reader** folder.
3. Double-click the **INVENTORY** file. It will open in Notepad.
4. Note the pattern of data types: There is a string field followed by three numeric fields. Examination of the fields reveals the following:
   - The first field is a string that is almost certainly an article of clothing.
   - The second field is numeric and contains 5 digits.
   - The third field is numeric and contains 5 digits.
   - The fourth field is numeric and contains 4 digits.
5. Click the **File** menu, and then click **Exit**. Notepad and the file will close.

Inspection alone rarely discloses all you need to know about a data file. For example, observation does not reveal that the second and third fields represent currency. Furthermore, even if you know that the those fields *are* currency, there is nothing in the file to tell you whether the amount shown as 01995 is $19.95 or $1,995. Inspecting a file in advance can tell you a lot, but it will not necessarily tell you *everything*. However, the file description shown in *Logic*, Figure 4-2 is clear: The fields are described, and the second and third fields, in particular, are shown to have two decimal places. Therefore, 01995 should be interpreted as $19.95.

EXAMINING THE INVENTORY READER CODE

Before examining the code for the Inventory Reader solution, you will duplicate the solution and then, as always, you will open the duplicate rather than the original. Work through the following steps:

1. Duplicate the **Inc Inventory Reader** folder located in the **ch04** folder in your student files.
2. Rename the duplicate from **Copy of Inc Inventory Reader** to **Inventory Reader**.
3. Open the **Inventory Reader** folder, and then double-click either the **Inventory Reader** solution or the **Inventory Reader** project. It will open in VB .NET.
4. If you are not in the Code window, click **Form1.vb** in the **Solution Explorer** window, then click the **View** menu, and then click **Code**.

The solution consists of a single procedure, the `Form1_Load` procedure, shown in Table 4-1. The line numbers in the table are not part of the procedure but have been added for reference purposes.

TABLE 4-1: THE INVENTORY READER FORM1_LOAD PROCEDURE

```
1       Private Sub Form1_Load(ByVal sender As System.Obj...
2           'housekeeping
3
4           While Not EOF(1)
5               'mainLoop: read record
6
7
8
9
10              'mainLoop: add field to list
11
12          End While
13          'finishUp
14
15      End Sub
```

Notice the remarks in Table 4-1: They indicate where the housekeeping, the two mainLoop tasks, and the finishUp are to be coded, and they correspond to the tasks discussed earlier in this chapter. When coding a procedure based on a flowchart or pseudocode, if you begin by coding remarks that correspond to the flowchart shapes or the pseudocode, not only will you ensure that no steps are left out of your procedure, but also you will make your code easier for others to understand. In Table 4-1, notice also the line spaces (the blank lines) under the remarks. These are the places where your code will be entered. Your code will accomplish the following tasks:

- Line 3 is where you will type the instruction to open the file.
- Line 4 corresponds to the EOF decision in the flowchart. It is the beginning of the loop. This particular loop, called a WHILE loop, was introduced in Chapter 2 of the *Logic* textbook and will be discussed in Chapter 7 of this textbook. WHILE there is data to read, the solution executes the tasks in the `mainLoop` routine. Once the EOF has been reached, the solution "drops out of the loop" and executes the `finishUp` routine.
- In lines 6 through 9, you will enter the instructions to read the four fields that comprise each record in the file. This is the first of the two tasks in the `mainLoop` routine.
- In line 11, the item name will be added to the items in the list box that appears on the form. This is the second of the two tasks in the `mainLoop` routine.
- Line 12, `End While`, marks the end of the loop. It simply tells the procedure to return to line 4.
- Line 14 is where the file will be closed.
- Line 15 marks the end of the procedure.

HOW THE EOF FUNCTION WORKS

Visual Basic makes use of a file pointer to read data. When a file is opened, the file pointer points to the first item of data. When that item of data is read, the pointer points to the second item of data, and so on, as the solution reads through the whole file. When the last item of data is read, the file pointer points to the end of the file.

When a solution calls the `EOF` function, `EOF` reads the FILE POINTER and returns a *False* if the file pointer is still pointing to data—or a *True* if the pointer is pointing to the end of the file. Your solution uses `Not EOF` to control the loop. As long as EOF is *not* true, the solution will execute the statements that are inside the loop. Once EOF becomes true, the solution drops out of the loop and closes the file.

COMPLETING THE PROCEDURE

Now that you understand the steps in the procedure, only the actual coding remains. The following steps will walk you through this task:

1. If you are not in the Code window, click the **View** menu, then click **Code**.

2. At the top of the Code window, change the comments in the heading: The title can remain as it is, but replace the words **Your Name** with your own name or initials. Replace the word **Date** with the current date.

3. Under the **'declare variables** remark, there are four line spaces. You will need four variables to accommodate the four fields in the file. The variable names can be those provided in the *Logic* textbook in Figure 4-8, but you must use Visual Basic data types. Thus, instead of declaring them as *char, num, num, num*, as indicated in the *Logic* textbook, you will declare them as *string, decimal, decimal, integer*. Enter the following:

```
Dim invItemName As String
Dim invPrice As Decimal
Dim invCost As Decimal
Dim invQuantity As Integer
```

4. In the line space under the **'housekeeping** remark, enter the following instruction to open the file: **FileOpen (1, "INVENTORY.txt", OpenMode.Input)**

5. As discussed in Chapter 3, when working with a sequential file, a whole record must be read even though only one field is required for the solution. In the four line spaces under the **'mainLoop: read record** remark, enter the following:

```
Input (1, invItemName)
Input (1, invPrice)
Input (1, invCost)
Input (1, invQuantity)
```

6. Add the item name to the list by entering the following code in the line under the **'mainLoop: add field to list** remark: **lstDisplay.Items.Add (invItemName)** (IMPORTANT: The first letter in lstDisplay is a lowercase "L" and not the numeral one.)

7. In the line space under the **'finishUp** remark, enter the following instruction to close the file: **FileClose (1)**

SETTING THE VALUE OF A PROPERTY

Program solutions make use of objects, which include forms, buttons, labels, text boxes, etc. Each of these objects has properties that describe it. For instance, a text box has a name, a height, and a width. Properties have **default values**, or settings, that can be changed at design time or at run time. In the following practice activity, you will examine the objects in the Inventory Reporter solution and then change some of the property values.

1. Click the **View** menu and then click **Designer**. Notice three objects: First, there is the form. On it are two more objects known as **controls**. The white rectangle in the center of the form is a list box; the object near the bottom of the form is a button.

2. Click the button, and notice that the word **Button1** appears in the **Object Name** box, which is at the top of the Properties window (Figure 4-2).

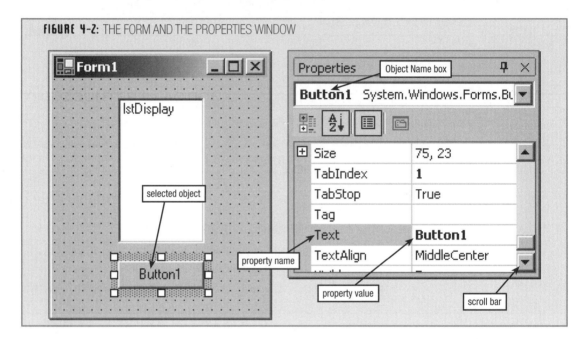

FIGURE 4-2: THE FORM AND THE PROPERTIES WINDOW

3. Scroll through the **Properties** window until you reach the **Text** property. The button's text property still has its default value, which is Button1. Change the value of the **Text** property from **Button1** to **Exit**. Notice that the button on the form now shows **Exit** rather than **Button1**. Also notice that the **Object Name** box still shows **Button1**—you changed the *text* property, not the *name* property. An object's text property is what the user sees when a form is in run time.

4. Scroll up to the **(Name)** property. The button's name property still has its default value, which is Button1. Change the **(Name)** property from **Button1** to **btnExit**. Notice that the **Object Name** box now shows **btnExit**. An object's name property is what a programmer uses when referring to the object in a procedure.

5. Click the list box on the form and notice its name: The name property was originally the default, **ListBox1**, but the programmer changed it to **lstDisplay**. Incidentally, don't bother to look for a list box's text property: A list box doesn't have one. Instead, it has an **Items** property that is not a single value, but a list. When the solution runs, the procedure will input data from the file and then output selected data items to the list.

6. Notice the title bar at the top of the form—it displays the word **Form1**. Click the form itself, that is, the gray area surrounding the other objects. In the **Properties** window, scroll to the form's text property and notice that it still shows its default value, **Form1**. (Make sure you are looking at the *text* property and not the *name* property, which is also **Form1**.) Change the value of the *text* property from **Form1** to **Inventory Reader**. Notice that the change is reflected in the form's title bar.

CREATING YOUR OWN PROCEDURE

The solution is almost finished. You completed the procedure that executes when the form loads. Now you must write the procedure that executes when the user clicks the `Exit` button. The following steps will show you how:

1. Double-click the **Exit** button. The Code window opens to reveal a procedure header and footer with a blinking insertion point between them (Figure 4-3).

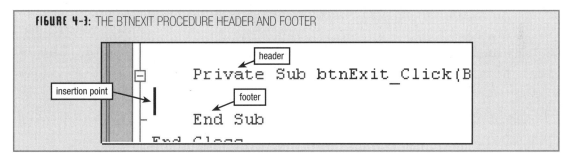

FIGURE 4-3: THE BTNEXIT PROCEDURE HEADER AND FOOTER

2. Type **Me.Close** and then click somewhere else in the Code window. VB .NET will indent your words and insert a set of parentheses after Me.Close. When the solution is running, this procedure will have the same effect as clicking the close box at the top right corner of a window: When the user clicks the *Exit* button, the window will close and the solution will end.

3. Test your solution by clicking the **Debug** menu, and then clicking **Start**. After a several moments, your form will appear on the screen (Figure 4-4).

FIGURE 4-4: THE INVENTORY READER FORM IN RUN TIME

4. Click the **Exit** button on the form. Your solution should end.

5. Quit VB .NET by clicking the **File** menu and then clicking **Exit**.

CHAPTER SUMMARY

Your solution in this chapter read a whole file and output the data from one of the fields in the file. In the next chapter, you will process, or modify, the data before outputting it. Chapter 4 presented these key points:

- ❑ It is a good practice to write procedure comments that correspond to the flowchart or pseudocode on which the procedure is based.

- ❑ The EOF function returns a *True* when the last item of data in a file has been read.

- ❑ Objects have properties that have default values. The values can be changed in the Properties window.

- ❑ The Visual Basic Properties window consists of an Object Name box, a list of property names, and their corresponding values.

- ❑ The text property of an object is what a user sees when a solution is running. The name property is what a programmer uses to reference the object in a procedure.

REVIEW QUESTIONS

Complete each sentence with a term from the list. Some of the terms will not be used.

1. **A property's setting is its _____.**

2. **At the top of the properties window is a list box which shows the object's _____.**

3. **Before creating a procedure that reads a sequential file, you should examine the file to discover the _____ used for each field.**

4. **Commas and carriage returns are used to _____, or separate, the data items in a sequential file.**

5. **The _____ function checks to see if the data in a file has been read.**

a. data types
b. delimit
c. EOF
d. method
e. name
f. value
g. TLA
h. field

EXERCISES

Use what you have learned in this chapter to work through the following exercises.

1. **Campers Reader**

    a. Open the **Inc Campers Reader** folder located in the **ch04** folder in your student files.

    b. Open the **bin** folder that is inside the **Inc Campers Reader** folder and examine the **CAMPERS** file. Note the number of fields.

    c. Duplicate the **Inc Campers Reader**, and then rename the duplicate from **Copy of Inc Campers Reader** to **Campers Reader**. Open either the **Campers Reader** solution or the **Campers Reader** project.

    d. In the **Designer** window, change the appropriate property value so that the words **Campers Reader** appear in the title bar of the form.

    e. Create a procedure for the **Exit** button that ends the solution when the user clicks the button.

    f. In the **Code** window, place your own name and the current date in the heading.

    g. Run the solution. Notice that it displays all the data in the file; in fact, in order to view the complete output, you must use the scroll bar at the side of the list box on the form. There is a logic error. The programmer wanted the solution to display just the last names of the campers. Modify the **Form1_Load** procedure to produce the desired output.

2. **Students Reader**

    a. Open the **Inc Students Reader** folder located in the **ch04** folder in your student files.

    b. Open the **bin** folder that is inside the **Inc Students Reader** folder and examine the **STUDENTS** file.

    c. Duplicate the **Inc Students Reader** folder and then rename the duplicate from **Copy of Inc Students Reader** to **Students Reader**. Open the **Students Reader** solution or the **Students Reader** project. The steps that follow are the same as those you completed in the section titled *Completing the Procedure*, earlier in this chapter.

    d. In the *heading* region at the top of the Code window, enter your name or initials and the date, just as you did in *Completing the Procedure*, Step 2.

    e. As you did in Step 3 of *Completing the Procedure*, declare four variables to correspond to the four fields in the STUDENTS file. Choose appropriate variable names, and make sure the data types match those in the file.

    f. Under the **'housekeeping** remark, open the file as you in Step 4 of *Completing the Procedure*. However, in this exercise, the filename is **STUDENTS.txt**. (Don't forget to place it in quotation marks.)

    g. Under the **'mainLoop: read record** remark, input the four fields as you did in *Completing the Procedure*, Step 5.

    h. Under the **'add to list** remark, add the first name to the list box as described in Step 6 of *Completing the Procedure*.

    i. Under **'finishUp**, close the file as shown in Step 7 of *Completing the Procedure*.

    j. Run the solution: You should see eight names, beginning with "David" and ending with "Eduardo."

3.   **Employees Reader**

   a. Open the **Inc Employees Reader** folder located in the **ch04** folder in your student files. Open the **bin** folder that is inside the **Inc Employees Reader** folder and examine the **EMPLOYEES** file. The first field is the employee's ID number. The last field is the employee's hourly pay rate. The pay rate has two assumed decimal places, as discussed in *Logic*, Chapter 3.

   b. Duplicate the **Inc Employees Reader** folder and rename the duplicate from **Copy of Inc Employees Reader** to **Employees Reader**. Open the **Employees Reader** solution or the **Employees Reader** project.

   c. If the form is not visible, click **View**, then click **Designer**.

   d. Change the word that is shown on the button from **Button1** to **Exit**.

   e. Change the word in the form's title bar from **Form1** to **Employees Reader**.

   f. Click the **View** menu, then click **Code**. Use the instructions in the section titled *Completing the Procedure* that appeared earlier in this chapter as a guide in completing the remaining steps in this exercise.

   g. In the *heading* region at the top of the Code window, enter your own name or initials and the current date.

   h. In the *variables declaration* region, declare variables to correspond to the fields in the EMPLOYEES file. Use appropriate variable names and correct data types.

   i. Under **'housekeeping** open the file.

   j. Under **'mainLoop: read record** input the data.

   k. Under **'mainLoop: add to list** add the last name of the employee.

   l. Under **'finishUp** close the file

   m. Run the solution. There should be a list of names from "Washington" to "Bush," but because there are 43 employees, you will have to scroll to see them all. If you decide to print using the instructions in Appendix B, realize that the complete list will not be printed, but only that portion of the list that appears in the window. We will deal with this matter in a later chapter.

MODULARIZING A SOLUTION

In this chapter, you will learn how to do the following:

- ☐ Code a solution that has been subdivided into modules
- ☐ Distinguish between event handlers, general procedures, and functions
- ☐ Use the *= Operator
- ☐ Pass arguments to procedures and functions

In Chapter 4, a data-processing flowchart was implemented in a single procedure. In this chapter, each process shown in the flowchart will have its own procedure. Up until now, your procedures have all been *event handlers*. In this chapter, you will use general procedures and functions as well. In Chapter 4, you input a whole file, but you displayed only one field. In this chapter, with the help of some procedures composed expressly for the purpose, you will display several fields, formatted according to a print chart. In addition, you will be able to print a report from within the solution—you won't have to rely on the PrintScreen key described in Appendix B. To prepare for this chapter, you should have read the first four chapters of Joyce Farrell's textbook, *Programming Logic and Design, Third Edition*.

TWO KINDS OF PROCEDURES

In the last chapter, a whole solution was contained in a single procedure. The housekeeping, mainLoop, and finishUp tasks were all lumped together. This is of no consequence if the solution is a short and simple one, but for longer, more complicated solutions, the practice is to be avoided. This point is explained in Chapter 3 of the *Logic* textbook, which not only emphasizes the importance of modularizing a program, but also describes the process by which one procedure (called a "module" in the *Logic* textbook) can call another.

In VB .NET, solutions are modularized by placing each task in a procedure of its own. These procedures are called **general procedures** because they are not connected to any events or objects, as is the case with event handlers. General procedures do not respond to particular events; rather, they wait to be "called" by other procedures.

In the following practice activity, you will run two versions of the averaging program shown in *Logic*, Figure 3-4. The first version consists of a single procedure, while the second, modularized version consists of four procedures.

> TIP □ □ □ □ | These demonstration programs contain some things you haven't seen before: Each has a form that contains no controls, and they employ input boxes and message boxes. If you can ignore these things for now and focus on the remarks in the procedures, you will be able to see the program flow, and how it differs in the two solutions.

Work through the following steps to run and examine the first solution:

1. Open the **Unmodularized Averaging Program** folder located in the **ch05** folder in your student files.
2. Double-click either the **Unmodularized Averaging Program** solution or the **Unmodularized Averaging Program** project. It will open in VB .NET.
3. Click the **Debug** menu, and then click **Start**.
4. Follow the instructions as they appear on your screen. Enter numbers as prompted and click **OK** as directed.
5. When the solution ends, bring the **Code** window into view. If necessary, click the **View** menu, and then click **Code**.
6. Notice that there is only one procedure. The remarks are shown in sequence, beginning with `'getInput` and ending with `'displayResult`.
7. Click the **File** menu, and then click **Exit** to exit VB .NET.

In the second part of this activity, you will run and examine the modularized version of the same solution. Work through the following steps:

1. Open the **Modularized Averaging Program** folder located in the **ch05** folder in your student files.
2. Double-click either the **Modularized Averaging Program** solution or the **Modularized Averaging Program** project. It will open in VB .NET.
3. Click the **Debug** menu, and then click **Start**.
4. As you did when running the previous solution, follow the instructions as they appear on your screen, enter numbers when prompted, and click **OK** as directed.
5. When the solution ends, bring the **Code** window into view. If necessary, click the **View** menu, and then click **Code**.
6. Notice that this modularized solution consists of four different procedures, and that the word `Call` is used to jump from the `Form1_Load` procedure (the *Logic* textbook refers to this as the "main program") to the general procedures. When the general procedures have finished their work, the "main program" resumes execution where it left off.
7. Exit VB .NET.

In a modularized program solution, the main procedure is like a music conductor: It plays no instrument itself, but it "calls" on the other musicians in the proper sequence to perform their solos. In the modularized version of the averaging program, `Form1_Load` begins by calling `getInput`. When `getInput` is finished, `Form1_Load` calls the next procedure, which is `calculateAverage`, and so on, until all the procedures have been called and the solution is finished.

CODING A MODULARIZED SOLUTION

Writing code for a modularized solution is no different from writing code as you have been doing. As a matter of fact, the solution in the following practice activity is quite similar to the Inventory Reader solution that you completed in the previous chapter. Work through the following steps:

1. Open the **Inc Inventory Report** folder located in the **ch05** folder in your student files.
2. Open the **bin** folder that is inside the **Inc Inventory Report** folder and double-click the **INVENTORY** file. It will open in Notepad.
3. Note that the file is the same one you worked with in Chapter 4. Recall that the second and third fields, which contain 5 digits each, should be interpreted as having two decimal places; for example, the number 01995 is to be interpreted as 19.95. Although this matter could be ignored in Chapter 4, it must be dealt with in this solution.
4. Exit **Notepad** and **INVENTORY**.
5. Duplicate the **Inc Inventory Report** folder, and rename the duplicate from **Copy of Inc Inventory Report** to **Inventory Report**.

6. Open the **Inventory Report** folder, and double-click either the **Reporter** solution or the **Reporter** project. It will open in VB .NET.

7. Open the **Code** window, and in the *heading* region of the solution, replace the words **Your Name** with your own name or your initials. Replace the word **Date** with the current date.

8. In the *variables declaration* region, notice that four variables have already been declared. You may recognize the names, which are the same as those used in the Inventory Reader solution for Chapter 4. However, because the purpose of this solution is to calculate the profit, an additional variable is needed. In the line space below **invQuantity**, enter the following declaration: **Dim profit As Decimal**

9. Locate the procedure header titled **Private Sub housekeeping**, and notice that it contains remarks for three tasks.

   a. Under the **'open file** remark, the task has already been coded.

   b. Under the **'display title** remark, type the following: **lstDisplay.Items.Add ("Inventory Report")** (Remember that the first letter in `lstDisplay` is a lowercase "L" and not the numeral one.) Recall from Chapter 4 that this instruction adds whatever is in parentheses to the list that will appear in the list box on the form.

   c. Delete the remark that reads **'display column headings**. Column headings won't be needed in this particular solution.

10. Scroll to the header that reads **Private Sub mainLoop**. The `mainLoop` procedure consists of three tasks.

    a. Under the **'read record** remark, four lines have already been coded. They will read the four fields from the INVENTORY file and assign the data to the variables shown.

    b. Under the **'process data** remark, you will add two decimal places to the price and to the cost (i.e., you will convert 01995 to 19.95). Then you will calculate the profit by subtracting the cost from the price. Enter these three lines:

```
invPrice *= 0.01
invCost *= 0.01
profit = invPrice - invCost
```

    c. Under the **'display results** remark, add the profit to the list of items that will be displayed by typing the following: **lstDisplay.Items.Add (profit)**

11. In the **finishUp** procedure, take out the words "Your Name" and key in your own name or initials. (Keep the quotation marks and the parentheses.)

12. Run the solution. Your output should match that shown in Figure 5-1, except that your own name or initials should appear.

13. Click the **Exit** button on the form to stop the solution, but do not close it. In the next practice activity, you will modify the Inventory Report.

FIGURE 5-1: OUTPUT FROM FIRST INVENTORY REPORT

FIGURE 5-1: OUTPUT FROM FIRST INVENTORY REPORT

```
Inventory Report
Inventory Report
5.38
3.25
116.5
3.3
Ellen W.
```

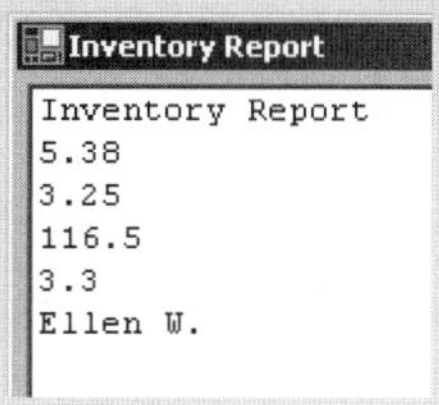

Note that the output in Figure 5.1 shows a list of profit amounts for the items in the file.

COMBINING AN ARITHMETIC OPERATOR WITH AN EQUALS SIGN

As you typed the previous solution, perhaps you were puzzled by the line `invPrice *= 0.01`. You know what an equals sign (=) is, and perhaps you also know that the asterisk (*) is the sign used for multiplication, but using them together as an operator might be new to you. `invPrice *= 0.01` instructs the computer to take the value of `invPrice`, multiply it by `0.01`, and then use the result as the new value for `invPrice`.

Here's another example: Consider a variable `intCounter` that has a current value of `17`. After the statement `intCounter += 1` the value of `intCounter` will be `18`. Combining an operator with an equals sign can be used not only for mathematical operations but also for strings, and you will encounter it from time to time throughout this textbook.

THE OUTPUT FROM THE REPORT

Admittedly, the report shown in Figure 5-1 is not impressive, but at least the calculation of the profit is accurate. The retail selling price for the first clothing item is 19.95 and its wholesale cost to produce is 14.57; therefore, the profit is 19.95 minus 14.57, or 5.38, and so on for the other items whose profit was displayed in Figure 5-1. The output could be improved if the numbers were expressed in dollars and cents. You can accomplish this by using a *function*.

FUNCTIONS

A **function** is a general procedure that returns a value to the procedure that called it. The calling procedure frequently—but not always—assigns the returned value to a variable. Consider a calling procedure containing the statement `decSmall = Math.Min(3, 11)`. The instruction calls the `Math.Min` function and passes it two numbers, 3 and 11. The function determines which is smaller and returns the value, 3. The calling procedure then assigns the value 3 to the variable `decSmall`. A function does not necessarily have to return a number: Depending on what the function was designed to do, it can return any kind of information as a value. Although this function and the others you will be using in this textbook are built into Visual Basic, it is possible to write your own functions, and writing one is no more difficult than writing a procedure.

There is an additional aspect of both functions and general procedures that needs to be introduced at this point: When a calling procedure passes a piece of information to a function or a procedure, that piece of information is referred to as an **argument**. Some functions and procedures require no arguments, while others require several. In the example in the preceding paragraph, the `Math.Min` function requires two arguments—it needs two numbers to compare. When arguments are passed from a calling procedure to a function, they must be enclosed in parentheses, and if several arguments are passed, they must be separated from one another by commas. Hence, the `Math.Min` function syntax is `( 3 , 11 )`: The two arguments are enclosed in parentheses and separated from one another by a comma.

USING A FUNCTION

To have your output expressed in dollars and cents, you will call the `FormatCurrency` function. The `FormatCurrency` function requires one argument. Its argument will be the value of the `profit` variable. The `FormatCurrency` function will transform the number into a string that begins with a dollar sign ($) and includes two decimal places for the cents. When the string is returned, the calling procedure—in this case, the `mainLoop` procedure—will add it to the list of items in `lstDisplay` rather than placing it into a variable. In the following steps, you will modify `Inventory Report` to include this function.

1. Under the **'display results** remark, replace the line **lstDisplay.Items.Add (profit)** with **lstDisplay.Items.Add (FormatCurrency(profit))**

2. Run the solution. Your output should match that shown in Figure 5-2, except that your own name should appear. The output is not much improved from the earlier version, but at least there are dollar signs.

3. Click the **Exit** button on the form to stop the solution, but do not close it. In the next activity, you will transform Inventory Report into a more presentable report.

FIGURE 5-2: FORMATTED OUTPUT FROM INVENTORY REPORT

```
Inventory Report
Inventory Report
$5.38
$3.25
$116.50
$3.30
Ellen W.
```

THE REPORTER PROCEDURES

You may already have noticed that your code window contains two lines, `Reporter Declarations` and `Reporter Procedures`, that were not present in earlier solutions. These are hidden regions of code that will facilitate the formatting of output.

 TIP ☐ ☐ ☐ ☐ | There is nothing secret about these hidden regions—the idea is merely to get them out of the way. If you like, you can examine the code by clicking the plus signs to the left of the lines. The plus signs will become minus signs, and the code will be exposed. To hide the code again, click the minus signs.

Three hidden procedures, `Splice`, `displayLine`, and `insertLineSpace`, are used to create a report. All three are general procedures that are called from various places in your solution. The `Splice` procedure is used to build up a line of text for the report. When you are finished composing the line, `displayLine` adds it to the report. From time to time, you need to skip a line in a report—`insertLineSpace` does exactly that. The following steps will show you how to use these procedures:

1. In **housekeeping** under the **'display title** remark, replace the single line that reads, **lstDisplay.Items.Add("Inventory Report")** with the following three lines:

```
Call Splice ("Inventory Report", C, 32)
Call displayLine()
Call insertLineSpace()
```

In the code that you just added, `Splice` requires three arguments: The first is the string to be displayed. In this case, the string consists of the words *Inventory Report*. The second argument is a letter—either *L*, *R*, or *C*—to indicate the alignment. If you choose *L*, the leftmost letter (in this case, the letter "I" of *Inventory*) is placed at position 32. If you choose *R*, the rightmost letter (the letter "t" in *Report*) is placed at position 32. Because you entered *C*, the title will be centered at position 32. The third and last argument for the `Splice` procedure is a number between 1 and 64 that indicates the print position. The formatting procedures have been set up to accommodate 64 letters on a line; therefore, 32 is the midpoint of the line. The next procedure, `displayLine` takes no arguments. It adds the line you just created to the report. Likewise, `insertLineSpace` takes no arguments. It simply adds a line space to the report.

2. Returning to your coding chores, in **mainLoop**, under the **'display results** remark, replace the line that reads **lstDisplay.Items.Add (FormatCurrency(profit))** with the following three lines:

```
Call Splice (invItemName, L, 15)
Call Splice (FormatCurrency(profit), R, 50)
Call displayLine()
```

Because both the item's name and its profit are to appear on the same line, `displayLine` is not called until both strings have been spliced. Notice that right-alignment is used when displaying numbers—right-alignment lines up the digits and decimal points.

3. In **finishUp**, under the **'display author name** remark, replace the line that displays your name with the following three lines (Type your own name or initials instead of "Ellen W".):

```
Call insertLineSpace()
Call Splice ("by Ellen W", R, 64)
Call displayLine()
```

Here, you want to skip a line between the body of the report and your own name; hence, you begin by calling `insertLineSpace`. The arguments passed to `Splice` specify right alignment at position 64. This will place your name flush with the right margin of the page.

4. Run your completed solution. The report should look like the one shown in Figure 5-3.

FIGURE 5-3: FULLY FORMATTED INVENTORY REPORT

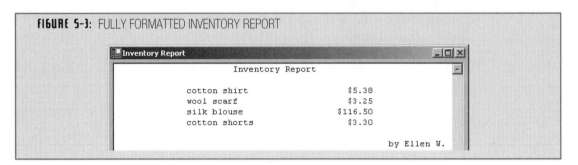

5. Make sure you have access to a printer, then click the **Print** button at the bottom of the form. Your report should print.

6. Click the **Exit** button on the form to stop the solution.

7. Exit VB .NET.

CHAPTER SUMMARY

This chapter has provided you with the tools to create and print modest reports for the exercises in the remaining chapters of this textbook. The following key points were presented:

☐ A modularized solution often makes use of a "main program" or main procedure that does nothing more than call the other procedures in the solution.

☐ An event handler, also known as an event procedure, executes in response to some event. A general procedure executes in response to a call from another procedure. A function is a general procedure that returns a value to the calling procedure.

☐ An arithmetic or string operator can be combined with an equals sign to change the value of a variable. An example is X += Y, where the value of X is increased by the value of Y.

☐ Arguments that are passed to procedures or functions must be enclosed in a single set of parentheses and separated from one another by commas.

REVIEW QUESTIONS

Select the term or phrase that best completes each sentence.

1. _____ **is a procedure that returns a value or piece of information.**
   a. A called procedure
   b. A function
   c. A general procedure
   d. An event handler

2. _____ **is a procedure that executes in response to an event.**
   a. A subroutine
   b. A triggered function
   c. An event function
   d. An event handler

3. **A piece of information that is passed to a function or procedure is known as** _____.
   a. a literal
   b. a value
   c. a variable
   d. an argument

4. **When several pieces of information must be passed to a function or procedure, they must be separated from one another by _____.**

   a. commas

   b. parentheses

   c. an *= operator

   d. remarks

5. **If `intCost = 1995` and you want to change the value to 19.95, use _____.**

   a. `Format Currency(intCost)`

   b. `intCost *= .01`

   c. `intCost *= intCost * .01`

   d. `FormatCurrency(intCost * .01)`

6. **In the VB .NET code window, a plus sign in the left margin indicates that a region of code has been _____.**

   a. disabled

   b. deleted

   c. hidden

   d. moved from another location

7. **In the procedure `determineCookingTime ("Asparagus", .25, Wt, Cals)` _____ arguments are passed to the procedure.**

   a. two

   b. three

   c. four

   d. an indeterminate number of

8. **In the modularized solutions discussed in this chapter, most of the work was done by _____.**

   a. the main program

   b. the general procedures

   c. the event handlers

   d. the functions

EXERCISES

Exercise: Student Report

1. Open the **Inc Student Report** folder located in the **ch05** folder in your student files.

2. Open the **bin** folder that is inside the **Inc Student Report** folder, and double-click the **STUDENTS** file. It will open in Notepad.

3. Examine the data. You may notice that STUDENTS contains the same information as Chapter 1, Exercise 3, in the *Logic* textbook. Determine how many fields there are in the file and what data types are involved. Choose the variable names you want to use, and then close Notepad and the STUDENTS file.

4. Duplicate **Inc Student Report** folder located in the **ch05** folder in your student files, and change the name of the duplicate from **Copy of Inc Student Report** to **Student Report**.

5. Open the **Student Report** folder, then double-click either the **Reporter** solution or the **Reporter** project. The solution will open in VB .NET.

6. In the Designer window, change the title that appears in the form's title bar from **Reporter** to **Student Report**.

7. In the *heading* region of the **Code** window, change the solution title from **Reporter 2.7** to **Student Report**. On the following line, replace the word **'Date** with the current date. (Remember to keep the apostrophe.)

8. In the *variables declaration* region, declare variables to hold the data from the **STUDENTS** file.

9. In the **housekeeping** procedure, under the **'open file** remark, replace the words **"path and filename.txt"** with **"STUDENTS.txt"**

10. Under the **'display title** remark, replace the words **"Report Title"** with **"Student Report"**

11. Under the **'display column headings** remark, enter the following six lines:

    ```
    Call Splice ("Last Name", L, 4)
    Call Splice ("First Name", L, 20)
    Call Splice ("Major", L, 35)
    Call Splice ("GPA", R, 60)
    Call displayLine()
    Call insertLineSpace()
    ```

12. In the **mainLoop** procedure, under the **'read record** remark, enter the statements to read the data from the file and assign them to variables. Use the variable names you declared earlier, and make sure you read the data items in the same order in which they are stored in the file.

13. In **mainLoop**, under the **'display results** remark, enter the five lines shown below. However, substitute your own variable names for the ones shown.

    ```
    Call Splice (TheLastNameVar, L, 4)
    Call Splice (TheFirstNameVar, L, 20)
    Call Splice (TheMajorVar, L, 35)
    Call Splice (TheGPAVar, R, 60)
    Call displayLine
    ```

14. In the **finshUp** procedure, under the **'display author name** remark, replace the words **"your own name"** with your own name or initials.

15. Run your solution. The output should appear like the one shown in Figure 5-4, except that it should display your own name or initials.

16. If desired, click the **Print** button on the form to print the report.

17. Click the **Exit** button to stop the solution.

FIGURE 5-4: OUTPUT FROM STUDENT REPORT

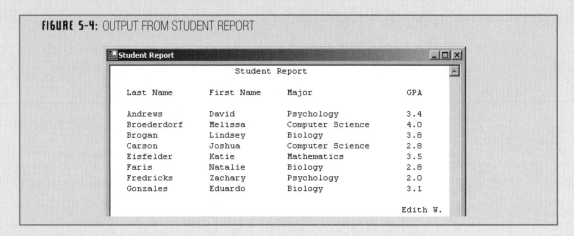

MAKING DECISIONS

In this chapter, you will learn how to do the following:

- ☐ Code dual-alternative and single-alternative selections
- ☐ Code AND and OR operators in selections
- ☐ Use a case structure
- ☐ Use nested IFs

In this chapter, your solutions will make decisions about the information that is read from a file. You will continue to follow the data-processing paradigm presented in Chapter 4, and you will continue to use the Reporter procedures presented in Chapter 5. Appendix D contains instructions on how to use the Reporter. Because every activity in this chapter uses the Reporter, it is wise to read Appendix D before working through the practice activities. To prepare for this chapter, you should have read Chapter 5 of Joyce Farrell's textbook, *Programming Logic and Design*, *Third Edition*.

CODING A DUAL-ALTERNATIVE SELECTION

Visual Basic .NET supports all the decision structures discussed in *Logic,* Chapter 5, and you will find that VB .NET syntax is practically identical to the pseudocode shown in *Logic*. The first decision structure, a "dual-alternative selection," is illustrated in Figure 5-3 of the *Logic* textbook. Complete the following steps to calculate a payroll:

1. Open the **ch06** folder in your student files. Inside it is the **Inc Payroll Report** solution folder that you need for this activity. The Inc Payroll Report solution folder contains a **bin** folder, and inside the bin folder is the **PAYROLL DATA** file that is used in this activity. Follow the instructions in **Appendix D**, then proceed to Step 2 of this activity.

2. In the **Code** window, the *variables declaration* region lists six variables, but the **PAYROLL DATA** file has only five fields. The first five variables will receive their values from the file, but the sixth, **grossPay**, will be calculated.

3. The housekeeping procedure has already been coded for you, but notice under the **'display column headings** remark that three columns of information will be displayed.

4. In the **mainLoop** procedure, under the '**process data** remark, code the following lines. Notice that the code is practically identical to the pseudocode shown in *Logic,* Figure 5-3. (Incidentally, you can ignore the indenting—VB .NET will indent for you.)

```
If hoursWorked > 40 then
    grossPay = 40 * rate + (hoursWorked - 40) * 1.5 * rate
Else
    grossPay = hoursWorked * rate
End If
```

5. In **mainLoop**, under the **'display results** remark, key in the following four lines of code, which will place the employee's last name, first name, and gross pay in a single line. Notice that the print positions are the same as those for the column headings shown in the housekeeping procedure. Notice also that **grossPay** is formatted as currency. (The `FormatCurrency` function was discussed in Chapter 5.)

```
Call Splice (strLastName, L, 15)
Call Splice (strFirstName, L, 30)
Call Splice (FormatCurrency(grossPay), R, 53)
Call displayLine()
```

TIP □ □ □ □ | *Rule of Thumb*: Calculate first, then display. The remarks in this activity direct you to `process data` before you `display results`. If you were to reverse the order, `grossPay` would be zero. In Visual Basic, when numeric variables are declared, they are assigned a default value of zero. If your solution displays before it calculates, all the user will see is the default value.

6. Run your solution. The first few lines of output should look like those shown in Figure 6-1. Because the output is rather long, you will need to use the scroll bar on the list box to view the complete report.

7. Do not exit. The next practice activity is a continuation of this one.

FIGURE 6-1: FRAGMENT OF PAYROLL REPORT, BEFORE DEDUCTIONS

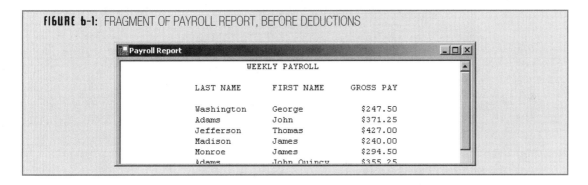

CODING A SINGLE-ALTERNATIVE SELECTION

A "single-alternative selection" is illustrated in *Logic*, Figure 5-4. The selection determines whether the employee is enrolled in the company dental plan. If the `dentalPlanCode` is "Y" (for "yes"), then $23.50 is deducted from the employee's gross pay. This selection is implemented in the following steps, which are a continuation of the previous practice activity.

8. In the **mainLoop** procedure, below the **End If** that you coded in the previous practice activity and above the **'display results** remark, enter the following four lines of code. Because this is an additional calculation, it too must be placed before the display instructions.

```
'calculate dental
If dentalPlanCode = "Y" Then
    grossPay -= 23.5
End If
```

9. Notice the following four details:
   • There is no `Else` in the selection block you just coded, hence the designation "single-alternative" selection.
   • In the second line that you coded, the letter "Y" must be uppercase: A computer treats "Y" and "y" as different letters.

- If you type 23.50, as shown in *Logic*, Figure 5-4, VB .NET will change it to 23.5 because the trailing zero is redundant.
- In the third line, the minus sign followed by an equals sign (- =) indicates that 23.5 is to be subtracted from `grossPay`, and the result is to become the new value for `grossPay`. (This is equivalent to typing `grossPay = grossPay - 23.5`.)

10. Run your solution. The first few lines of output should look like those shown in Figure 6-2.

FIGURE 6-2: FRAGMENT OF COMPLETED PAYROLL REPORT

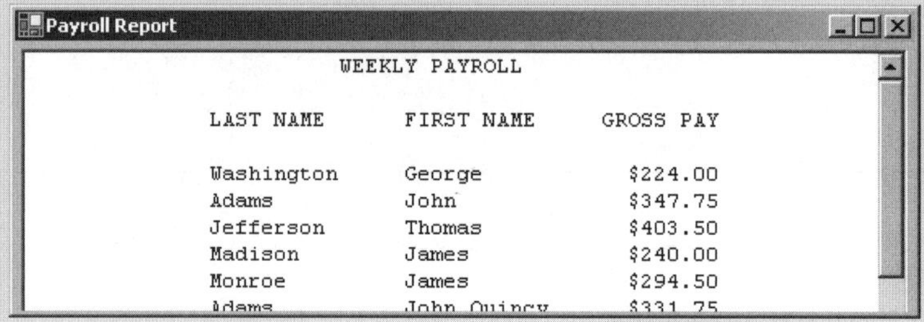

CODING AN AND OPERATOR

In Chapter 5 of *Logic*, beginning at about Figure 5-8, an insurance report is discussed. After demonstrating the selection process using nested IF statements, the selection is implemented using the AND operator. You will code an AND operator in the following steps:

1. In the **ch06** folder in your student files is the **Inc Insurance Report** solution folder that you will need for this activity. The Inc Insurance Report solution folder contains a **bin** folder, inside of which is **EMPFILE**, a data file that is used in this activity. Follow the instructions in **Appendix D**, and then proceed to Step 2 of this activity.

2. In the *variables declaration* region, notice that the variable names are the same as those shown in *Logic*, Figure 5-12, except for the column headings. *Logic* treats the column headings as variables (*char heading1* and *char heading2*), but the Reporter solutions do not.

3. The print chart for **Insurance Report** is found in *Logic*, Figure 5-10. Notice that the first line on the print chart is not used. The title appears on the second line in print position 4.

4. In the **housekeeping** procedure, under the **'display title** remark, code the following four lines, which will display the report title as shown in the print chart:

```
Call insertLineSpace()
Call Splice("Employees with Medical and Dental Insurance", L, 4)
Call displayLine()
Call insertLineSpace()
```

5. In **housekeeping**, under the **'display column headings** remark, code the following:

```
Call Splice("ID number", L, 4)
Call Splice("Last name", L, 22)
Call Splice("First name", L, 44)
Call displayLine()
Call insertLineSpace()
```

6. In the **mainLoop** procedure, under **'select and display**, code the decision described in *Logic*, Figure 5-17, as shown in the following six lines. Note that the AND operator will ensure that the report shows only those employees who have *both* medical *and* dental insurance.

```
If empDentalIns = "Y" And empMedicalIns = "Y" Then
    Call Splice (empIdNumber, L, 4)
    Call Splice (empLastName, L, 22)
    Call Splice (empFirstName, L, 44)
    Call displayLine()
End If
```

7. Run your solution. The first few lines of output should look like those shown in Figure 6-3.
8. The next activity is a continuation of this one and involves changing what you have already coded. If you intend to print out the report and/or the code for what you have done so far, *do it now*, before going on.

FIGURE 6-3: FRAGMENT OF INSURANCE REPORT USING AND

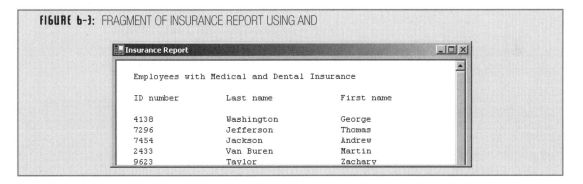

CODING AN OR OPERATOR

The syntax of AND statements and that of OR statements is practically identical: The difference between this solution and the previous one is a single word. Change that word in two places, as indicated in the following steps:

9. In **housekeeping**, under **'display title**, change the word **and** to **or** in the report's title.
10. In **mainLoop**, in the line immediately beneath the **'select and display** remark, change the word **And** to **Or** in the selection statement (the IF statement).

11. Run your solution. The first few lines of output should look like those shown in Figure 6-4. The output shows employees who have *either* medical *or* dental insurance (or both).

```
Insurance Report                                    _ □ ×

    Employees with Medical or Dental Insurance

    ID number        Last name          First name

    4138             Washington         George
    5184             Adams              John
    7296             Jefferson          Thomas
    3249             Madison            James
    5359             Monroe             James
    6395             Adams              John Quincy
    7454             Jackson            Andrew
    2433             Van Buren          Martin
    2517             Tyler              John
    6621             Polk               James K.
    9623             Taylor             Zachary
```

USING A CASE STRUCTURE

As the *Logic* textbook points out, when a selection involves several possible alternatives based on the value of a single variable, a case structure is more convenient than a series of IF-THEN-ELSE structures. In the following practice activity, you will use a case structure to implement the flowchart shown in *Logic,* Figure 5-37.

1. In the **ch06** folder in your student files is the **Inc Real Estate Report** solution folder that you will need for this activity. The Inc Real Estate Report solution folder contains a **bin** folder, inside of which is **HOUSE MODELS**, a data file that is used in this activity. Follow the instructions in **Appendix D**, then proceed to Step 2 of this activity.

2. In the *variables declaration* region, notice three variables. The variables `strAddress` and `strModel` will receive their values from the data file. The value of the variable `intBasePrice` will be determined by the house model that is selected. Notice the data type for the price: Normally, the data type for currency would be *decimal*, but in this case, the data type for `intBasePrice` can be *integer* because the report involves only whole dollars.

3. In **mainLoop**, under **'determine price'**, code the following case selection:

```
Select Case strModel
    Case "Arlington"
        intBasePrice = 150000
    Case "BelAire"
        intBasePrice = 170000
    Case "Carrington"
        intBasePrice = 185000
```

```
        Case Else
            intBasePrice = 0
    End Select
```

4. Run your solution. The output should look like Figure 6-5.

FIGURE 6-5: REAL ESTATE REPORT

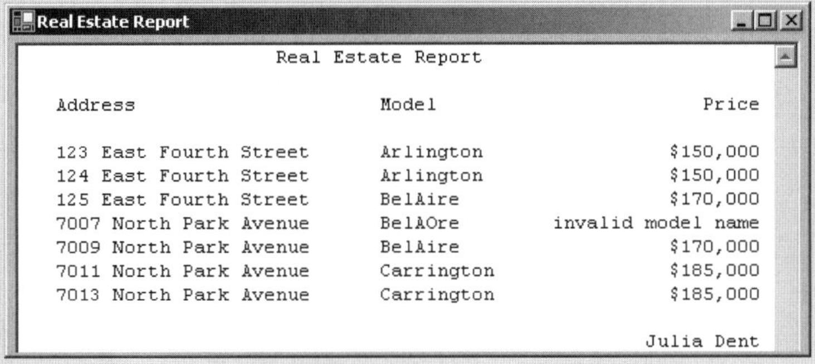

```
Real Estate Report                                          _ □ ×
                        Real Estate Report

    Address                      Model                    Price

    123 East Fourth Street       Arlington            $150,000
    124 East Fourth Street       Arlington            $150,000
    125 East Fourth Street       BelAire              $170,000
    7007 North Park Avenue       BelAOre      invalid model name
    7009 North Park Avenue       BelAire              $170,000
    7011 North Park Avenue       Carrington           $185,000
    7013 North Park Avenue       Carrington           $185,000

                                                     Julia Dent
```

Note the Error message in Figure 6-5. Because the "BelAOre" model is not listed as one of the cases, the case structure determines its base price to be zero (*Logic* refers to this as the "default" value). Then, in the `display results` routine, the IF statement indicates that if the base price is zero, display the error message.

There is one more detail that you may have noticed in the code for the display routine: In the line, `Call Splice (FormatCurrency(intBasePrice,0)`...etc., the `FormatCurrency` function received two arguments instead of only one. The second argument is optional: When present, it determines how many digits are to appear to the right of the decimal point. If the second argument is not present, `FormatCurrency` defaults to two decimal digits. Because real estate prices are always expressed in whole dollars, displaying two zeros for cents would detract from the report; therefore, `FormatCurrency` was instructed to format the `intBasePrice` with no digits to the right of the decimal point.

NESTED SELECTIONS

In *Logic* Chapter 5, immediately before Figure 5-38, find the section titled, "Using Decision Tables." That section describes how a decision table can be used to determine residence hall assignments. The discussion culminates in the flowchart shown in *Logic*, Figure 5-47. The following activity will implement that flowchart:

1. In the **ch06** folder in your student files is the **Inc Residence Hall Report** solution folder that you will need for this activity. The Inc Residence Hall Report solution folder contains a **bin** folder, inside of which is **STURESFILE**, a data file that is used in this activity. Follow the instructions in **Appendix D**, then proceed to Step 2 of this activity.

2. In the *variables declaration* region, you can see that the variable names are the same as those listed in *Logic*, Figure 5-47, and the data types are those described in *Logic*, Figure 5-38.

3. In the housekeeping procedure, the title and column headings are laid out as described in *Logic,* Figure 3-39.

4. In the **mainLoop** procedure, under the **'process data** remark, enter the following nested IF statements. (You can ignore the indenting—VB .NET will handle it for you.)

```
If stuAge < 21 Then
    If stuQuietRequest = "Y" Then
        assignedHall ="Addams"
    Else
        assignedHall = "Grant"
    End If
Else
        assignedHall = "Lincoln"
End If
```

You can see from the preceding code that younger students (under 21 years of age) are assigned to either Addams Hall or Grant Hall, depending on whether they want a quiet residence, but adult students (21 years of age or older) are assigned to Lincoln Hall.

5. In **mainLoop**, under '**display results**, enter the following three lines:

```
Call Splice(stuId, L, 4)
Call Splice(assignedHall, L, 17)
Call displayLine()
```

6. Run your solution. The output should look like that shown in Figure 6-6, except your own name should be shown.

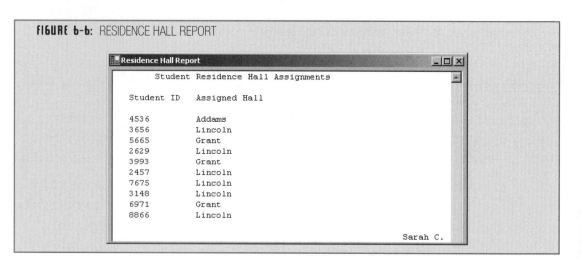

FIGURE 6-6: RESIDENCE HALL REPORT

CHAPTER SUMMARY

This chapter has illustrated the syntax for several kinds of selection structures supported by Visual Basic .NET. The following points were illustrated in the chapter's practice activities:

☐ Selection statements begin by testing a condition (or testing several conditions), the result of which is either true or false.

☐ A dual-alternative selection performs one action if the result of the condition test is true and a different action if it is false.

☐ A single-alternative selection performs an action if the result of the condition test is true, but performs no action if the result is false.

☐ For selections involving AND, both (or all) conditions must be true to yield a *true* result.

☐ For selections involving OR, only one of the conditions must be true (or both can be true) to yield a *true* result.

☐ When a selection involves several possible alternatives based on the value of a single variable, a case structure is more convenient than a series of IF-THEN-ELSE structures.

EXERCISES

The following exercises are based on the End of Chapter Exercises found in *Logic,* Chapter 5. Refer to *Logic* for descriptions of the data files and for instructions regarding what information should be present in the reports.

1. In the **ch06** folder in your student files is the **Inc Best Candy** solution folder that you will need for this exercise. The Inc Best Candy solution folder contains a **bin** folder, inside of which is **CANDY DATA**, the data file that is used in this exercise. Follow the instructions in **Appendix D**, and then use the instructions in *Logic*, Chapter 5, Exercises, Number 2 to prepare the report. The first few lines of output should be similar to that shown in Figure 6-7.

FIGURE 6-7: FRAGMENT OF BEST-SELLING CANDY REPORT

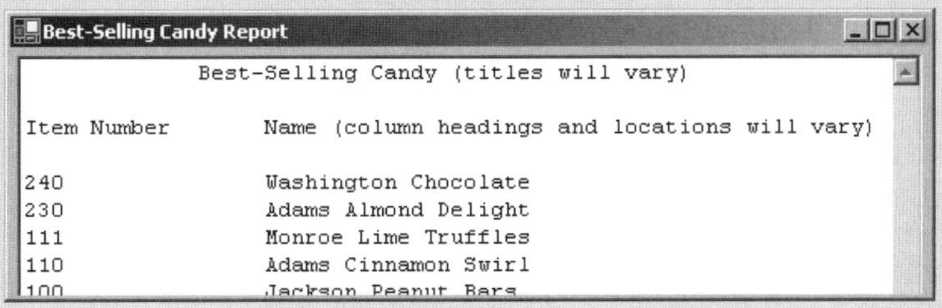

2.   In the **ch06** folder in your student files is the **Inc Expensive Candy** solution folder that you will need for this exercise. The Inc Expensive Candy solution folder contains a **bin** folder, inside of which is **CANDY DATA**, the same data file that was used in Exercise 1. Follow the instructions in **Appendix D**, and then create a report that displays the name and price of all candy that sells for more than ten dollars a pound. The output should be similar to that shown in Figure 6-8. Note that some of the names have been truncated, or trimmed. According to the data description in *Logic*, Chapter 5, Exercises, Number 2, the names of the candies do not exceed 20 characters in length.

FIGURE 6-8: EXPENSIVE CANDY REPORT

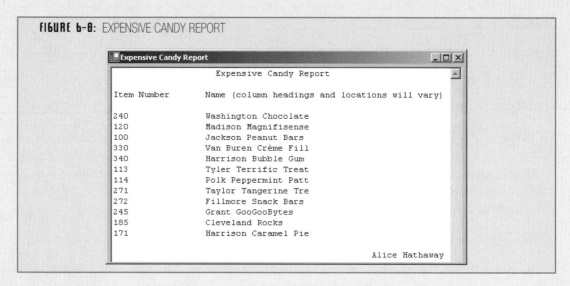

3.   In the **ch06** folder in your student files is the **Inc Honor Society Report** solution folder that you will need for this exercise. The Inc Honor Society Report solution folder contains a **bin** folder, inside of which is **CANDIDATES**, the data file that is used in this exercise. Follow the instructions in **Appendix D**, and then use the instructions in *Logic*, Chapter 5, Exercises, Number 4 to prepare the report. The output should be similar to that shown in Figure 6-9.

FIGURE 6-9: LITERARY HONOR SOCIETY REPORT

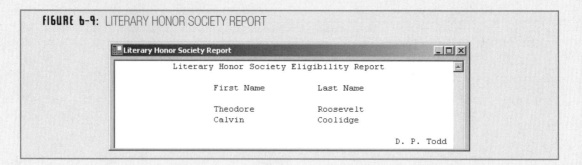

4. The Literature Classics Club want to recruit new members and would like a list of students from the CANDI-DATES file whose major is either English or Philosophy. In the **ch06** folder in your student files is the **Inc Classics Club Report** solution folder that you will need for this exercise. The Inc Classics Club Report solution folder contains a **bin** folder, inside of which is **CANDIDATES**, the same data file that was used in the previous exercise. Follow the instructions in **Appendix D** to begin your report. The output should be similar to that shown in Figure 6-10:

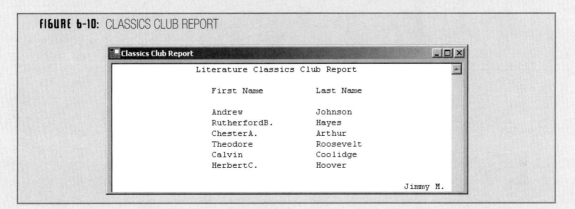

FIGURE 6-10: CLASSICS CLUB REPORT

EXPLORING LOOPS

In this chapter, you will learn how to do the following:

- [ ] Use a variable to control a loop
- [ ] Distinguish between local variables and module-level variables
- [ ] Identify the steps in loop structures
- [ ] Use a WHILE loop
- [ ] Use a DO UNTIL loop
- [ ] Use a FOR loop
- [ ] Concatenate strings

In Chapter 6, you learned how to format output using the Reporter solution. In this chapter, you will not need the Reporter because you will explore loops and create labels rather than create reports. However, the printer utility is still a component of every solution in this chapter, so you can obtain a hardcopy of your output, if desired. To prepare for this chapter, you should have read Chapter 6 of Joyce Farrell's textbook, *Programming Logic and Design*, *Third Edition*.

LOOPS

As the *Logic* textbook points out, a **loop** is a programming structure that allows the same block of code to be used several times. Loops must be controlled so the block of code does not repeat endlessly. In this textbook, you have been using a WHILE loop to read and display the information contained in a file, and your loops have been controlled by the EOF function. In this chapter, you will explore three kinds of loops: the WHILE loop, the DO UNTIL loop, and the FOR loop. You will control loops with a variable.

The loops explored in this chapter have common steps that each must follow: They all involve a **counter**, which is a variable that must be initialized, incremented or decremented, and must be compared with an ending value. In addition, there is a **loop body**, which is where the actual computing work takes place. These terms are defined in Chapter 6 of the *Logic* textbook, and they will be illustrated as you work through the practice activities in this chapter.

THE WHILE LOOP

Your first practice activity involves a WHILE loop that is based on *Logic*, Figure 6-2. However, instead of printing the word "warning" four times, as shown in *Logic*, it will print your name. Work through the following steps:

1. Duplicate the **Inc Repeater** folder that is inside the **ch07** folder in your student files.
2. Rename the duplicate from **Copy of Inc Repeater** to **Repeater**.
3. Open the **Repeater** folder, and then double-click either the **Repeater** solution or the **Repeater** project. It will open in VB .NET
4. In the **Designer** window, examine the form. Notice that it has `Print` and `Exit` buttons. The procedures for these buttons have already been coded. Also notice that the form contains a list box named `lstDisplay`. This list box is smaller than the one you used in the Reporter solution because no reports will be created, but it serves the same purpose—to display the output from the solution.
5. Examine Table 7-1. The line numbers in the left column and the comments in the right column have been added for reference purposes. You will type the code statements in the middle column of the table, but first, let's look at the code more closely.

TABLE 7-1: A WHILE LOOP

1	`Private Sub Form1_Load (ByVal sender As Sys ...`	1 procedure header
2	`    Dim rep As Integer`	2 declare loop counter
3	`    rep = 1`	3 initialize loop counter
4	`    While rep < 5`	4 compare to ending value
5	`        lstDisplay.Items.Add ("M. Todd")`	5 loop body
6	`        rep += 1`	6 loop body: increment
7	`    End While`	7 end of loop
8	`End Sub`	8 procedure footer

THE WHILE LOOP CODE

Lines 3 through 7 in Table 7-1 correspond to the flowchart and pseudocode shown in Figure 6-3 of the *Logic* textbook. Lines 1, 2, and 8 in the table are required by VB .NET, but they are not shown in *Logic*.

- Line 1 in Table 7-1 identifies the procedure as a `Form_Load` event handler, that is, a procedure that executes as soon as the form is called into memory.

- Line 2 declares the variable that will serve as the loop counter. Variables that are declared inside a procedure, as `rep` is, are referred to as a **local variables**, and they can only be used by the procedure in which they are declared. Typically, loop counters are local variables. By contrast, **module-level variables** (which are akin to the "global variables" mentioned in the *Logic* textbook) are declared outside of procedures and can be used by any procedure in the Code window. Incidentally, the lines of code in a code window comprise a *module*, hence the term, *module-level* variable. It is a convention in VB .NET that module-level variables are declared in the region immediately above the first procedure that is coded, as you have been doing up to now.

TIP □ □ □ □ | For an example of a module-level variable, consider the `lastName` variable that you declared in the Payroll Report in Chapter 6. Because you declared it in the *variables declaration* region above the first procedure, it was able to be used by both the `mainLoop` and the `Splice` procedures.

- Line 3 initializes the counter by assigning it a value of `1`.

- Line 4 compares the counter to the ending value, `5`. When the value of the counter is greater than 5, the procedure will "drop out of the loop" and proceed to line 8, which ends the procedure.

- Lines 5 and 6 are the loop body. This is where the actual work is done. In line 5, the name "M. Todd" is added to the list that is displayed on the form. (Remember that the first letter in `lstDisplay` is a lowercase "L" and not the numeral one.) In line 6, the counter is incremented by adding 1 to its value.

- Line 7 marks the end of the loop. It simply tells the procedure to return to line 4.

- Line 8 ends the procedure.

CODING THE PROCEDURE

Now that you understand the steps in the procedure, only the actual coding remains. Complete the following steps:

1. In the **Code** window of the **Repeater** solution, under the **Form1_Load** procedure header, enter the code as shown in Table 7-1. When you get to line 5, replace the name "M. Todd" with your own name or initials. Make sure to keep the quotation marks.

2. Run the solution. You should see your name displayed four times in the list box on the form.

3. Click the **Exit** button to stop the solution, but do not close it. Because you will be modifying this solution in the next practice activity, it is a probably a good idea to print out your code before going on. Click the **File** menu, and then click **Print**.

THE COUNTER IN ACTION

In this activity, you will display the value of the counter along with your name. You will accomplish this by **concatenating**, or joining, the two pieces of information.

1. In the **Code** window, replace the line **lstDisplay.Items.Add ("M. Todd ")** with **lstDisplay.Items.Add ("M. Todd " & rep)** (Your own name or initials should appear between the quotation marks.)

2. In the line you just typed, there should be a space between the last letter of your name and the quotation marks. (This is explained in the next section.) In addition, there should be a space before and after the ampersand (&).

3. Run your solution. Your display should be the same as that shown in Figure 7-1, except that your own name or initials should appear.

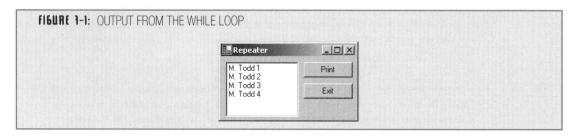
FIGURE 7-1: OUTPUT FROM THE WHILE LOOP

4. Click the **Exit** button to stop the solution. Print out your code by clicking the **File** menu, and then clicking **Print**.

5. Do not close the solution. The next practice activity is a continuation of this one.

CONCATENATION

Concatenation joins two or more items of information, turning them into a single string. For example, if the words "Here are " and the words "four words" are concatenated, they become the single string "Here are four words". In this example, there must be a space after the word "are " and the closing quotation mark. If it is omitted, when "Here are" is concatenated to "four words" the result is "Here arefour words". In VB .NET, the concatenation operator is the ampersand (&) sign.

In addition to joining strings, VB .NET also allows the concatenation of numbers: Thus, 3 & 2 & 1 is concatenated to 321. Although it is possible to use concatenation in this way, it is rarely useful to concatenate numbers.

THE DO UNTIL LOOP

A WHILE loop begins with a comparison; a DO UNTIL loop ends with one. That is the only difference between the two kinds of loops. In the next activity, you will turn your WHILE loop into a DO UNTIL loop. Work through the following steps:

1. Replace the line that reads, **While rep < 5** with the word **Do**
2. Replace the line that reads, **End While** with the words **Loop Until rep > 5**
3. Run your solution. Your display should be the same as that shown in Figure 7-2, except that your own name or initials should appear instead of *M. Todd*.
4. Click the **Exit** button to stop. Print your code, but do not close the solution. The next activity is a continuation of this one.

FIGURE 7-2: OUTPUT FROM THE DO UNTIL LOOP

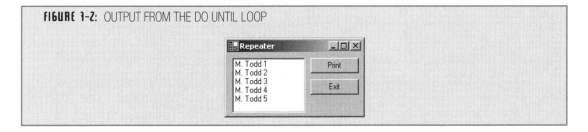

TIP ▫ ▫ ▫ ▫ Because your comparison indicated that the procedure should loop until `rep` was greater than 5, five names were displayed. If you were to change the ending value in the comparison line to read `Loop Until rep > 4`, your output would be identical to that of the WHILE loop.

THE FOR LOOP

The FOR loop is identical to the WHILE loop except that several steps are combined. Examine Table 7-2.

TABLE 7-2: A FOR LOOP

1	`Private Sub Form1_Load (ByVal sender As Sy ...`	1
2	`Dim rep As Integer`	2 declare loop counter
3	`For rep = 1 To 5`	3 initialize and compare
4	`lstDisplay.Items.Add ("M. Todd " & rep)`	4 loop body
5	`Next`	5 increment and loop
6	`End Sub`	6

- Line 3 of Table 7-2 assigns `rep` an initial value of `1` and then tests to see whether its current value is greater than `5`.

- Line 4 is the loop body. Unlike the WHILE and DO UNTIL loops, `rep` in the FOR loop does not have to be incremented in the loop body.

- Line 5 increments `rep` and then sends the procedure back to line 3.

- Back at line 3, `rep` is not reinitialized; rather, its current value is compared with the ending value `5`. Eventually, `rep` will be greater than `5`, at which time the procedure will drop out of the loop and proceed to line 6, which ends the procedure.

Work through the following steps to modify and test the Repeater solution with a FOR loop.

1. In the **Code** window of the **Repeater** solution, delete the six lines that you entered in the **Form1_Loop** procedure, and key in the code in Table 7-2. As you did in this chapter's first activity, ignore the left column containing the line numbers, ignore the right column with the comments, and type only the code that is in the middle column. As you did in the previous activities, replace the name "M. Todd " with your own name.

2. Run your solution. Your display should be the same as that shown in Figure 7-3, except your own name or initials should appear instead of the name *M. Todd*.

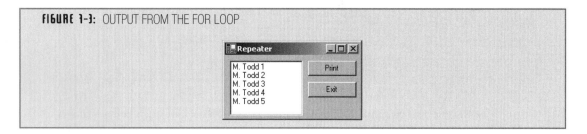

FIGURE 7-3: OUTPUT FROM THE FOR LOOP

THE LABEL MAKER PROGRAM

In the section titled "Using a Counter to Control Looping" in Chapter 6 of the *Logic* textbook, a WHILE loop is used to print employee labels 100 times. In the following activity, you will create the label maker, but for simplicity's sake, your solution will display the labels only five times for each name.

BEGINNING THE SOLUTION

As always, you will begin by examining the data file, duplicating a partially completed solution, and inserting your own name in the code.

1. Open the **Inc Label Maker** folder located in the **ch07** folder in your student files.

2. Open the **bin** folder that is inside the **Inc Label Maker** folder.

3. Double-click the **FIRSTNAMES** file. It will open in Notepad.

4. Notice that the file lists the first names of six employees. It consists of only one field, a string.

5. Click the **File** menu, and then click **Exit**. Notepad and the file will close.

6. Duplicate **Inc Label Maker** folder, and rename the duplicate from **Copy of Inc Label Maker** to **Label Maker**.

7. Open the **Label Maker** folder, and double-click either the **Label Maker** solution or the **Label Maker** project. It will open in VB .NET.

8. In the *heading* region at the top of the **Code** window, key in your name or initials and the current date in the two lines provided for that purpose.

9. In the **Form1_Load** procedure, notice that the code implements the flowchart in Figure 6-5 of the *Logic* textbook; that is, it calls the housekeeping, mainLoop, and finishUp procedures.

10. The housekeeping routine has been coded for you. It simply opens the file.

11. The **finishUp** procedure has been partially coded. Under the **'display author name** remark, replace the words "your own name" with your name or initials.

THE OUTER LOOP

Label Maker will contain a loop within a loop. The first, or outer, loop will read each employee's name in turn. The second, or inner, loop will print five labels using the employee's name. Work through the following steps to set up and test the outer loop:

1. In the **mainLoop** procedure, you will begin by declaring a variable for the name field. Because `mainLoop` is the only procedure that will need to use the variable, it can be declared as a local variable. Enter the following: **Dim strName As String**

2. Next, the mainLoop procedure will read an item of data from the file and assign it to the variable. Enter the following: **Input (1, strName)**

3. Finally, you will concatenate the phrase "made for you personally by " to the name and add the result to the list that will be displayed on the form. Enter the following:

   lstDisplay.Items.Add ("Made for you personally by " & strName)

4. Run your solution. Your display should be the same as that shown in Figure 7-4, except your own name or initials should appear at the very end.

5. Click the **Exit** button to stop the solution, but do not close it.

FIGURE 7-4: OUTPUT FROM LABEL MAKER, PART 1

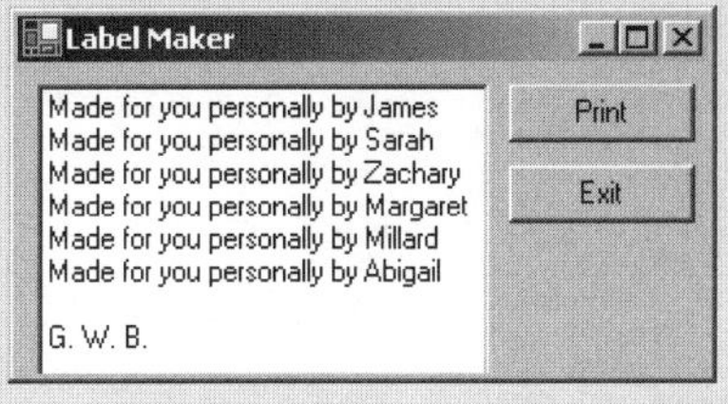

THE INNER LOOP

You have the outer loop running successfully: The solution loops to display a label for each name in the FIRSTNAMES file. To complete the solution, you will set up an inner loop to print each label five times. Work through the following steps:

1. In the **mainLoop** procedure, you will add to the three lines you already have (lines 2, 4, and 7) by keying in the code shown in Table 7-3. As you did in the earlier activities, key in just the middle column. When you get to line 7 in the table, make sure that it appears as one long line, not as the two separate lines shown.

TABLE 7-3: THE CODE FOR THE INNER LOOP

1	`Private Sub mainLoop( )`	1
2	`Dim strName As String`	2
3	`Dim intCounter As Integer`	3 declare loop counter
4	`Input (1, strName)`	4
5	`intCounter = 1`	5 initialize loop counter
6	`While intCounter < 6`	6 compare to ending value
7	`lstDisplay.Items.Add ("Made for you personally by " & strName)`	7 loop body: concatenate phrase and employee name
8	`intCounter += 1`	8 loop body: increment counter
9	`End While`	9 end of loop
10	`End Sub`	10

2. Run your solution. The output is too large for the form. To see the complete output, you must use the scroll bar on the side of the list box. The first few lines of output should be the same as that shown in Figure 7-5.
3. For a printout of your labels, click the **Print** button on the form. It will print out on a single page.
4. Stop your solution. For a printout of your code, click **File**, and then click **Print**.
5. Close the solution and exit VB .NET.

FIGURE 7-5: FRAGMENT OF OUTPUT FROM LABEL MAKER, COMPLETED

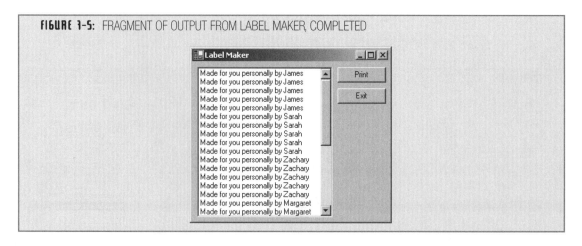

CHAPTER SUMMARY

This chapter has illustrated the syntax for three kinds of loops supported by Visual Basic .NET. The following points were illustrated:

- ☐ A loop is a programming structure that allows the same block of code, called the loop body, to be used several times.

- ☐ Three common types of loops are the WHILE loop, the DO UNTIL loop, and the FOR loop.

- ☐ A loop that is controlled by a variable must employ three steps: The variable is initialized. It is incremented or decremented. It is compared to an ending value.

- ☐ Module-level variables are declared outside of procedures—by convention, they are declared immediately above the first procedure. A module-level variable can be used by any procedure in the module, or Code window.

- ☐ Local variables are declared within a procedure—by convention, they are declared immediately below the procedure header. A local variable can be used only by the procedure in which it was declared.

- ☐ In a WHILE loop, the comparison to the ending value is made at the beginning of the loop. In the case of a DO UNTIL loop, the comparison is made at the end.

- ☐ A FOR loop is the same as a WHILE loop with several steps combined.

- ☐ Strings and numbers can be concatenated, or joined, by using the ampersand (&) character.

REVIEW QUESTIONS

Select the term or phrase that best completes each sentence.

1. **The first step in using a variable as a loop counter is to _____ it.**
   a. increment
   b. compare
   c. declare
   d. decrement

2. **In a FOR loop, the loop control variable is incremented _____ .**
   a. in the IF statement
   b. in the FOR statement
   c. in the NEXT statement
   d. in the loop body

3. **To control a loop, a loop counter variable is compared to _____ .**
   a. a counter
   b. the loop body
   c. the initialized value
   d. the ending value

4. **A DO UNTIL loop compares the loop control variable _____ .**

a. at the beginning of the loop
b. at the end of the loop
c. in the loop body
d. when the variable is first declared

5. **The concatenation operator is _____ .**

a. the ampersand
b. the plus sign
c. the pound sign
d. the asterisk

6. **A local variable _____ .**

a. is the same as a module-level variable
b. is the same as a global variable
c. can be used by several procedures
d. can be used by only one procedure

EXERCISES

1. Duplicate your **Label Maker** folder, the one containing your completed project, and rename the duplicate from **Copy of Label Maker** to **Label Maker DO UNTIL**. Modify your code to use a DO UNTIL loop to produce the same output as your original Label Maker.

2. Duplicate your **Label Maker** folder, the one containing your completed project, and rename the duplicate from **Copy of Label Maker** to **Label Maker FOR**. Modify your code to use a FOR loop to produce the same output as your original Label Maker.

3. Duplicate the **Inc Greeting** folder that is inside the **ch07** folder in your student files. Rename the duplicate from **Copy of Inc Greeting** to **Greeting**. Run the solution. The word **Hello** will be displayed. In the **Code** window, change the heading to show your own name and the current date. Use a WHILE loop to produce the output shown in Figure 7-6. Change the code under the **'add author name** remark, so the last line of the output shows your own name or initials instead of **J. F. K.**

FIGURE 7-6: OUTPUT FROM GREETING

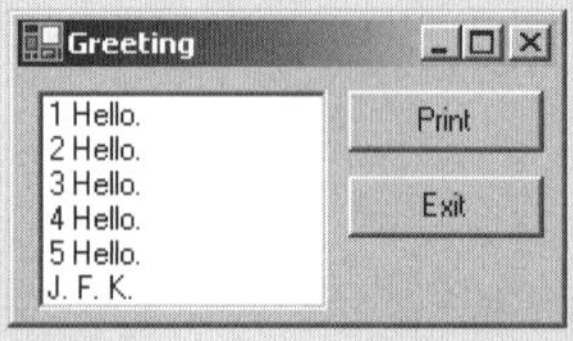

4. Duplicate the **Inc Greeting** folder once again. Rename the duplicate from **Copy of Inc Greeting** to **Greeting FOR**. Use a FOR loop to produce the same output as in the previous exercise.

8

EXPLORING ARRAYS

In this chapter, you will learn how to do the following:

☐ Distinguish between simple variables and arrays

☐ Use an accumulator

☐ Use a case structure for nested decisions

☐ Use an array in a solution

The previous chapters have all made use of simple variables. A **simple variable** holds one piece of data, and because of its unique name, it stands apart from the other variables used in a solution. In this chapter, you will make use of an array. An **array** is a list of variables that are related both by name and by the type of data they store. Each variable in an array is referred to as an **element**, and although each element holds but one piece of data, the data items are all related in some way. Therefore, a whole array contains a group of related data. To prepare for this chapter, you should have read the first eight chapters of Joyce Farrell's textbook *Programming Logic and Design, Third Edition*.

ACCUMULATING A TOTAL

The first scenario discussed in *Logic,* Chapter 8 requires the use of an accumulator, which is a simple numerical variable used to "run up," or accumulate, a total. An accumulator updates, or increments, its value in the same way as did the counter that you employed in Chapter 7. The main difference between the two is that a counter increases its value by a constant amount, but an accumulator increases its value from a variable. To see an example of an accumulator in action, do the following:

1. Open the **Accumulator Demo** that is in the **ch08** folder in your student files. It adds the numbers in the Five Primes file (the same Five Primes file that you worked with in Chapter 3).

2. Run the solution. You will see the two message boxes shown in Figure 8-1.

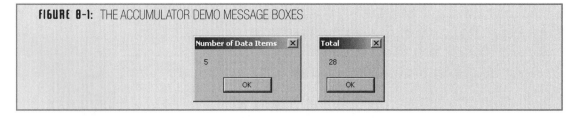

FIGURE 8-1: THE ACCUMULATOR DEMO MESSAGE BOXES

The value in the first message box (shown on the left) is the result of counting the number of data items in the file. Because there are five numbers in the file, it is no surprise that the count is 5. The value in the second message box (shown on the right) is the sum of all the data items. That is, 2+3+5+7+11 equal 28.

How does the solution arrive at the figures in the message boxes? Table 8-1 shows the three lines of code that comprise the main loop. The code is shown in the left column of the table. The explanation is in the right column.

TABLE 8-1: CODE FROM THE ACCUMULATOR DEMO SOLUTION

`Input (1, intPrime)`	The solution reads a number from the data file and assigns it to the variable `intPrime`.
`intCounter += 1`	The counter is increment by 1 (a *constant* amount).
`intTotal += intPrime`	The total is incremented by the value of `intPrime` (a *variable*).

USING AN ACCUMULATOR

In the following practice activity, you will use an accumulator to hold a running total of the cans collected in the recycling drive described in *Logic*, Chapter 8. After all the cans have been added to the total, the value of the accumulator will be displayed in a label.

1. Open the **Inc Total Cans** folder located in the **ch08** folder in your student files.
2. Open the **bin** folder that is inside the Inc Total Cans folder, and then double-click the **STURECORDS** file. It will open in Notepad.
3. Notice that the file is made up of two numerical fields. The description of STURECORDS found in *Logic,* Figure 8-2 indicates that the first field represents the student class—which, as *Logic* explains, is 1 for freshmen, 2 for sophomores, 3 for juniors, and 4 for seniors. The second field is the number of cans collected. Close the file and exit Notepad.
4. Duplicate the **Inc Total Cans** folder, and then rename the duplicated folder from **Copy of Inc Total Cans** to **Total Cans**.
5. Open the duplicated folder, and then double-click either the **Total Cans** solution or the **Total Cans** project. The solution will open in VB .NET.
6. Select the form by moving your mouse pointer to the **Solution Explorer** window, and then clicking **Form1.vb**. Once it is selected, click the **View** menu, and then click **Designer**.
7. Notice that the form uses a label for output instead of a list box. Because you have only one piece of information (total cans) to display and not a list of values, a list box is not required.
8. Click the label to select it, scroll through the **Properties** window, and notice the label's **Text** property and its **Name** property. You will use these properties later on in the activity.
9. Click the **View** menu, and then click **Code** to show the Code window.
10. In the *heading* region, replace the words **'Your Name** with your own name, and replace **'Date** with the current date.
11. In the *variables declaration* region, you will need three variables, all integers. The first two variables will obtain their values from the file. The third variable is the accumulator. Under the **'declare variables** remark, enter the following:

```
Dim intClass as Integer
Dim intCans as Integer
Dim intTotal as Integer
```

12. In the **'mainLoop** routine, under the **'read record** remark, two input statements are required: The first reads the class number; the second reads the number of cans. Although the class number is not used in this solution, it nevertheless has to be read as well. Enter the following:

```
Input (1, intClass)
Input (1, intCans)
```

13. In **'mainLoop**, under the **'accumulate total** remark, you will enter the line to build up the sum. Each time `intCans` acquires a new value, it will be added to `intTotal`. Enter the following: **intTotal += intCans**

14. In **'finishUp**, instead of using *Items.Add* as you did when you used a list box for output, you will use the *Text* property of the label. The label will display a sentence that you will assemble by concatenating three pieces of data: the beginning of the sentence, the variable, and a period. Under the **'display total** remark, enter the following: **lblDisplay.Text = "The total number of cans is " & intTotal & "."**

15. Run your solution. Your output should be the same as that shown in Figure 8-2.

16. Click the **Exit** button to stop the solution.

FIGURE 8-2: OUTPUT FROM THE TOTAL CANS SOLUTION

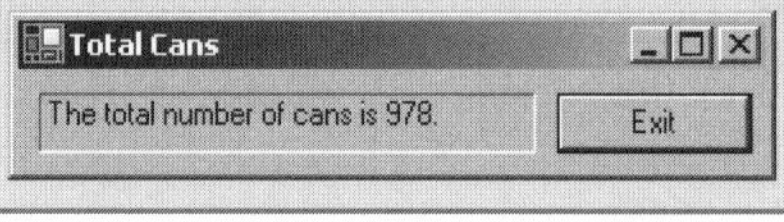

A CAN RECYCLING REPORT

The *Logic* textbook continues with the can-recycling scenario, and *Logic*, Figure 8-3 shows a print chart for a report that displays the total number of cans collected by each class. The *Logic* textbook goes on to discuss how the report can be generated, first by using nested decisions (see *Logic*, Figure 8-6), and then by using an array (see *Logic*, Figure 8-11). In the following activity, you will create that report using the case structure discussed in Chapter 6 of this textbook.

USING A CASE STRUCTURE FOR NESTED DECISIONS

When a selection involves several possible alternatives based on the value of a single variable, the case structure is a convenient way to handle the task. In this solution, the "single variable" is `intClass`, which will have a value of 1, 2, 3, or 4 (representing freshmen, sophomores, juniors, and seniors). Depending of the value of `intClass`, four alternative actions are possible. Work through the following steps to code the recycling report using a case structure.

1. Find the **Inc Recycling Report** solution folder that is in the **ch08** folder in your student files. The Inc Recycling Report solution folder contains a **bin** folder, inside of which is **STURECORDS**, the data file that is used in this activity. Follow the instructions in **Appendix D**, and then proceed to Step 2 of this activity.

2. In the *variables declaration* region, you will need six variables. You will use two of the variables for the fields in the data file. You will use the other four variables for the accumulators, one for each class. Under the **'declare variables** remark, enter the following:

```
Dim intClass as Integer
Dim intCans as Integer
Dim intTotal1 as Integer
```

```
Dim intTotal2 as Integer
Dim intTotal3 as Integer
Dim intTotal4 as Integer
```

3. Notice that the **housekeeping** procedure has already been coded for you. It opens the STURECORDS file and then displays the report title and headings shown in *Logic,* Figure 8-3.

4. In the **mainLoop** procedure, the input statements have been entered for you. (Notice that they are the same two input statements you used in the previous activity.)

5. In this step, the case selection block determines who gets credit for what. It will be analyzed at the conclusion of this practice activity. For now, under the **'accumulate totals** remark, enter the following (you can ignore the indenting—VB .NET will handle it for you):

```
Select Case intClass
    Case 1
        intTotal1 += intCans
    Case 2
        intTotal2 += intCans
    Case 3
        intTotal3 += intCans
    Case 4
        intTotal4 += intCans
End Select
```

6. The totals are not displayed until the finishUp procedure. In **finishUp**, under **'display total for class 1**, notice that three lines have already been coded (see Figure 8-2). It takes three lines to display a total for each class.

TABLE 8-2: EXCERPT FROM THE FINISHUP PROCEDURE	
`Call Splice("1", L, 4)`	Adds the class number, 1, to the current line of text that will be displayed (Class 1 is freshmen)
`Call Splice(intTotal1, R, 18)`	Adds the total cans for class number 1 to the current line of text that will be displayed
`Call displayLine()`	Adds the current line of text to the list box that will appear on the form, and then begins a new "current line"

7. In the **finishUp** procedure, beneath the three remaining **'display total** remarks, create the display for classes 2, 3, and 4, using the three lines shown in Table 8-2 as a model.

8. Run your solution to test it. Your output should look like that shown in Figure 8-3, except that your own name should appear.

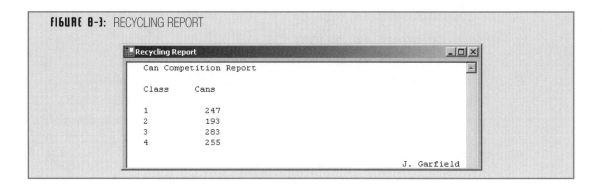

FIGURE 8-3: RECYCLING REPORT

THE CASE SELECTION CODE BLOCK

How does the case selection block of code determine who gets credit for what? Look at the first few records in the STURECORDS file, as shown in Figure 8-4.

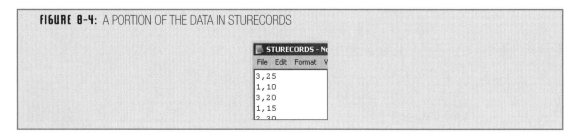

FIGURE 8-4: A PORTION OF THE DATA IN STURECORDS

When the first record is read, the data items are assigned to the variables as follows: $intClass$ = 3 and $intCans$ = 25. Once the variables have their values, the case structure can be employed. The case structure compares the value of $intClass$ (which has a value of 3) to Case 1. The result of the comparison is *False* (no match), so the case structure compares the value of $intClass$ to Case 2. Again, it is *False*. When the case structure compares the value of $intClass$ to Case 3, the result of the comparison is *True*; consequently, the 25 cans (i.e., the current value of $intCans$) are credited to $intTotal3$, which holds the total for the class of juniors (Class 3).

Next, the solution reads the second record, and assigns $intClass$ = 1 and $intCans$ = 10. The case structure compares the value of $intClass$ to Case 1. The result of the comparison is *True*; consequently, the 10 is added to $intTotal1$, which holds the total for the freshman class (Class 1).

Next, the solution reads the third record, assigning the 3 to $intClass$ and the 20 to $intCans$. As before, the case selection compares $intClass$ to Case 1 and then to Case 2, and the result of both comparisons is *False*. Case 3 evaluates to *True,* so the 20 (the current value of $intCans$) is added to the previous value of $intTotal3$, which was 25, bringing the current value of $intTotal3$ up to 45.

The solution continues in this manner. A record is read, and the two data items from the file are assigned to the variables. The case structure compares the value of $intClass$ to each of the cases, 1, 2, 3, and 4 in turn, and when it gets a match, it adds the value of the current $intCans$ to the appropriate class's total.

USING AN ARRAY

As discussed in *Logic,* Chapter 8, an array is a list of variables whose names are identical except for their subscript, which is also known as their **index**. The values that are stored in an array must all be of the same data type, and they should all be related. The array used in the following practice activity will be called `intTotal`. All its values will be integers, and the values are "related" in that each will represent the total number of cans collected by one of the high school classes.

In the following activity, the array will be declared as `intTotal(4)`, which means it will consist of five variables, or elements, from `intTotal(0)` through `intTotal(4)`. The first element, `intTotal(0)`, will not be used, so `intTotal(1)` will accumulate the number of cans collected by the freshman class. By the same token, `intTotal(2)` will represent the sophomore class, `intTotal(3)` will represent the junior class, and `intTotal(4)` will represent the senior class.

| In VB .NET, arrays are always created with an index starting with zero; therefore, if desired, you could store the totals for this solution in elements 0 through 3, rather than 1 through 4. The solution presented here wastes one "slot" in the array. However, wasting the zero element is not an uncommon practice, especially if it makes a solution easier to understand, as is the case here.

In the **STURECORDS** file, a portion of which is shown in Figure 8-4, the first field, which represents the class, will serve as the array index. The second field, which represents the number of cans collected by that class, will be added the value of the array variable.

By way of example, the following bulleted list shows how the proper class gets credit for the cans they collected:

- In the first row (the first record), the first field is 3; therefore, `intTotal(3)` will hold 25.
- In the second row, the first field is 1; therefore, `intTotal(1)` will hold 10.
- In the third row, the first field is 3; therefore, `intTotal(3)` will add 20 to the 25 it already holds, increasing its value to 45.
- In the fourth row, the first field is 1; therefore, `intTotal(1)` will add 15 to the 10 it already holds, increasing its value to 25, and so on through the whole file.

The following steps will generate the same can recycling report as the previous activity, only this time, it will be done using an array.

1. Find the **Inc Recycling Report Using an Array** solution folder that is in the **ch08** folder in your student files. It contains a **bin** folder, inside of which is **STURECORDS**, the data file that you used in the previous activity. You will not need to examine it again, but follow the other instructions in **Appendix D**, and then proceed to Step 2 of this activity.

2. In the *variables declaration* region, you will create two variables for the fields and an array to accumulate the totals. Code the following:

```
Dim intClass as Integer
Dim intCans as Integer
Dim intTotal(4) as Integer
```

3. In the **mainLoop** procedure, the input statements have been entered for you, but under the 'accumulate totals remark, enter **intTotal(intClass) += intCans**

4. In the **finishUp** procedure, you will set up a FOR loop to display your data. Enter the following code directly beneath the **Private Sub finishUp ()** procedure header:

```
'initialize local variable
Dim intIndex as Integer
'close file
FileClose(1)
For intIndex = 1 to 4
    'display class number
    Call Splice (intIndex, L, 4)
    'display class total
    Call Splice (intTotal(intIndex), R, 18)
    'The line is finished.
    Call displayLine()
Next
```

5. Run your solution to test it. Your output should look like that shown in Figure 8-3, except that your name should be displayed at the end.

CHAPTER SUMMARY

In this chapter, you used an accumulator and compared two ways to generate a report. The following key points were presented:

- ☐ An accumulator is a simple numeric variable that updates its value by using a variable.

- ☐ A counter is a simple numeric variable that updates its value by a constant increment.

- ☐ An array is a list of variables that are related both by name and by the type of data they store.

- ☐ An element is one variable in an array. Element names are identical except for their subscript, or index.

- ☐ A case structure is a convenient selection tool to use when a selection involves several possible alternatives based on the value of a single variable.

REVIEW QUESTIONS

Select the item that best completes each sentence.

1. **The symbols _____ can be used to increment a counter or update the value of an accumulator.**
   a. `:=`
   b. `+=`
   c. `& =`
   d. `=+`

2. **In the declaration `Dim intStatus(4) As Integer`, the number in parentheses _____ .**
   a. indicates the data type for the array
   b. indicates that the array consists of four variables
   c. indicates that the array consists of four elements
   d. indicates the highest subscript usable by the array

3. ***Subscript* and _____ are synonymous.**
   a. array
   b. superscript
   c. index
   d. counter

4. **Each element in an array must have _____ .**
   a. the same value
   b. a unique value
   c. the same data type
   d. the same subscript

5.   **In the statement** `intMore += intQuantity,` **the variable** `intMore` **is** _____ .
   a. a counter
   b. an accumulator
   c. an element
   d. a subscripted variable

EXERCISES

1.   Using an **IF** statement, modify the **Total Cans** solution that you created earlier in this chapter so it accumulates and displays only the cans collected by the sophomores (Class 2). The output should display 193.

2.   In the **Recycle Report Using an Array** solution, in the '**finishUp** procedure, change the statement that reads `For intIndex = 1 To 4` so it displays only the results for the sophomores and juniors. (It will accumulate totals for all four classes as it did previously. Only the display will be modified.)

3.   An elementary school consisting of grades 1 through 6 is conducting a can drive similar to the high school's drive. Using your completed **Recycle Report Using an Array** solution as a model, create a report for the elementary school. Begin by duplicating the **Inc Elementary Report** solution folder that is inside the **ch08** folder in your student files. Your output should look like that shown in Figure 8-5, except that your own name should appear at the end.

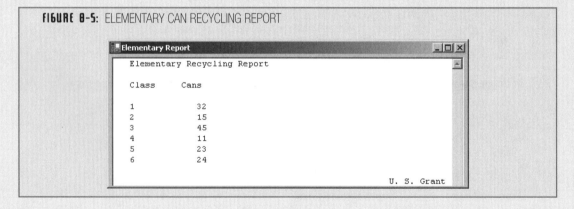

FIGURE 8-5: ELEMENTARY CAN RECYCLING REPORT

4.   Change the FOR loop in Exercise 3 so just grades 2 through 4 are displayed. (All six grades are accumulated; only the display will be different.)

MERGING SEQUENTIAL FILES

In this chapter, you will learn how to do the following:

- ☐ Compare a text file created in Notepad with one created by VB .NET
- ☐ Create and write to a sequential file
- ☐ Merge files to a list box
- ☐ Save merged data to a file

Thus far, you have **input** (or read) data from sequential files, and you have **output** data to list boxes and labels on a form. In this chapter, you will **output** (or write) data to a sequential file. In addition, instead of reading just one file at a time, you will read two files in the same solution and merge (combine) them. To get the most from this chapter, you should have read Chapter 11 in the Comprehensive Edition of Joyce Farrell's textbook, *Programming Logic and Design, Third Edition*. However, this chapter is complete in itself, and reading the *Logic* chapter is not a prerequisite.

READING AND WRITING SEQUENTIAL FILES

The sequential files that you have been working with are as easy to write to as they are to read from, but regardless of whether you write or read, you begin by opening the file and end by closing it. To read from a file, you use the keyword `Input` as you have been doing up to now, but to write to it, you use the keyword `Write`. Basically, that's the only difference.

COMPARING A VB .NET FILE AND A NOTEPAD FILE

The partially completed solution called **Sample** will give you a closer look at writing to a file. In the following practice activity, you will complete two procedures. The procedures are simple; consequently, you won't need separate house-keeping, mainLoop, and finishUp routines. As always, you will begin by examining the data files and then duplicating the solution folder. Work through the following steps.

1. Open the **Inc Sample** folder located in the **ch09** folder in your student files.
2. Open the **bin** folder that is inside the **Inc Sample** folder.
3. Double-click the **NAMEFILE** file. It will open in Notepad. Your screen should look like the window shown on the left side of Figure 9-1.

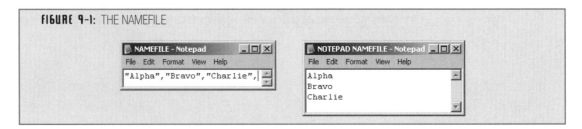

FIGURE 9-1: THE NAMEFILE

4. Exit Notepad. Go back to the **bin** folder and double-click **NOTEPAD NAMEFILE**. It, too, will open in Notepad. Your screen should look like the window shown on the right side of Figure 9-1.

The first file, **NAMEFILE**, was created by a VB .NET solution while the second, **NOTEPAD NAMEFILE**, is a Notepad document. As far as the computer is concerned, the two files are identical, even though they are different to human eyes. Notice the quotation marks and commas in the window on the left side of Figure 9-1. When VB .NET writes to a sequential file, it places quotation marks around strings and uses commas as delimiters to separate the data items. Although a typist could have created the Notepad document to look exactly like the VB .NET file, in this example, the quotation marks were omitted, and carriage returns were used instead of commas. Although the two files are *apparently* different, they are *logically* the same.

READING FROM A FILE

The next activity will demonstrate that the VB .NET file and the Notepad file are equivalent. Work through the following steps to code a procedure to read the files.

1. Exit Notepad if you have not already done so.
2. Duplicate the **Inc Sample** folder, and then rename the duplicate from **Copy of Inc Sample** to **Sample**.
3. Open the **Sample** folder, and then double-click either the **Sample** solution or the **Sample** project. It will open in VB .NET
4. Click **Form1.vb** in the **Solution Explorer** window, then click the **View** menu, and then click **Designer**. The Form will appear in the Designer window.
5. Notice the four controls: There is a list box named `lstDisplay` and three buttons named `btnRead`, `btnWrite`, and `btnExit`. The button `btnExit` that is used to stop the solution has already been coded, but you will write the procedures for `btnRead` and `btnWrite`.
6. Click the **View** menu, and then click **Code**. The Code window will appear.
7. Modify the heading at the top of the Code window to show your own name or initials and the current date on the lines provided for that purpose.
8. In the *variables declaration* region, notice that only one variable is needed and that it has already been declared as a string.
9. Under the **Private Sub btnRead** procedure header, code the following:

```
FileOpen(1,"NOTEPAD NAMEFILE.txt", OpenMode.Input)
While Not EOF(1)
     Input (1, strName)
     lstDisplay.Items.Add(strName)
End While
FileClose(1)
```

10. Run the solution. When the run-time form appears, click the **Read** button on the form. You should see the three names, **Alpha**, **Bravo**, and **Charlie**, on three separate lines in the list box.
11. Click the **Exit** button on the form to stop the solution.
12. Go to the **Code** window and in the **FileOpen** line, change the filename from **NOTEPAD NAMEFILE.txt** to **NAMEFILE.txt** (but keep the remainder of the line as it is).
13. Run the solution, and again, when the run-time form appears, click the **Read** button. You should see the identical three names: **Alpha**, **Bravo**, and **Charlie**.
14. Click the **Exit** button to stop the solution.

WRITING TO A FILE

As you discovered, the output from both files was the same, regardless of whether commas or carriage returns were used as delimiters. Next, you will write the code that outputs data to the NAMEFILE file.

1. Under the **Private Sub btnWrite** procedure header, code the following:

```
FileOpen(1,"NAMEFILE.txt", OpenMode.Output)
FileClose(1)
```

2. Scroll to the **Private Sub btnRead** procedure, and make sure that the filename is still **NAMEFILE.txt**.
3. Run the solution. When the run-time form appears, click the **Write** button, and then click the **Read** button. You should see nothing!
4. Click the **Exit** button to stop the solution.

Opening a file for output is a destructive operation. That is, if the file that you open for output already exists, all of its data will be destroyed as soon as you open the file for output. In this activity, you didn't actually write any information, so the data in **NAMEFILE** was replaced by nothing. Let's continue by actually writing some data to the file:

1. Go to the **Code** window, and in the **Private Sub btnWrite** procedure, between the **FileOpen** line and the **FileClose** line, enter the following three lines:

```
Write (1, 1)
Write (1, 2.345)
Write (1, "Six")
```

2. Run the solution. When the run-time form appears, click the **Write** button, and then click the **Read** button. You should see **1**, **2.345**, and **Six**, on three separate lines in the list box.
3. Click the **Exit** button to stop the solution, then click the **File** menu, and then click **Exit** to close the solution and exit VB .NET

In the previous activity, it was the VB .NET solution, not Notepad, that created the file. Therefore, there are certain things you can expect to see when you examine the data. Work through the following steps to check what your solution wrote.

1. Open the **bin** folder that is in your **Sample** folder, and then double-click **NAMEFILE**. It will open in Notepad.
2. Verify that the word "Six" is enclosed in quotation marks, but notice that the numbers are not. Verify also that the three data items are separated by commas.
3. Click the **File** menu, and then click **Exit**. Notepad and NAMEFILE will close.

In the next practice activity, you will read two files and then **merge**, or combine, them into a single list.

MERGING A CUSTOMER FILE

Merging sequential files is the first topic discussed in Chapter 11 of the *Logic* textbook. A file of East Coast customers is merged with a file of West Coast customers. Table 9-1 shows the names that are in the two files.

TABLE 9-1: CUSTOMER NAME FILES

East File	West File
Able	Chen
Brown	Edgar
Dougherty	Fell
Hanson	Grand
Ingram	
Johnson	

Your solution will merge the names from both files and will place the merged data in a list box in alphabetical order. According to the *Logic* textbook, there are two preconditions for merging. First, the files must have the same data structure. That is, they must have the same number of fields, and the data types for the fields must be identical. Second, the files must be sorted the same way, that is, they both must be in ascending or descending alphabetical order.

UNDERSTANDING THE MERGE

The purpose of this merge is to combine the names from both files into a single, alphabetized list. The solution's main loop will read a name from the East File into one variable, and a name from the West File into another. It will compare the two names, and the name that has the "lower alphabetical value" (the value closest to "A") will be added to the list box on the form.

Next, the variable that had the lower value will read a new name from its file, while the variable that had the higher value will retain its current name. A comparison will take place as before, and again the lower value will be added to the list box.

This loop—the process of reading, comparing, and adding to the list box—will continue until one file or the other runs out of data. When there is no more data to read, the out-of-data variable will be assigned a value of "ZZZZZ", which the *Logic* textbook refers to as a "high value," that is, a value greater than any possible value that could be used in the files.

As the solution continues to loop, the remaining file will continue to read and compare its data to the "ZZZZZ". Because each of those data items has a lower alphabetical value than "ZZZZZ", each, in turn, will be added to the list box. When the second file runs out of data as the first file did, the variable will be assigned a value of "ZZZZZ", and, because the values of *both* variables are "ZZZZZ", the solution will drop out of the loop and close the files. At this point, the merge is complete.

CODING THE MERGE

In the following practice activity, you will merge the two files shown in Table 9-1. It is not necessary to begin by examining the files because they are shown in the table, but you may feel free to do so if you wish.

1. Duplicate the **Inc Merge** folder that is inside the **ch09** folder in your student files.

2. Rename the duplicated folder from **Copy of Inc Merge** to **Merge**.

3. Open the **Merge** folder, and then double-click either the **Merge** solution or the **Merge** project. It will open in VB .NET.

4. In the *heading* region at the top of the **Code** window, key in your name or initials and the currrent date in the lines provided.

5. In the *variables declaration* region, notice that two string variables have been declared, `strEastName` and `strWestName`. These are the variables that will input their values from the East File and the West File, respectively.

6. In the **Form1_Load** procedure, notice that the loop condition has been changed. As noted in the previous section, the solution will loop until both variables have a value of "ZZZZZ". In other words, while either variable is not equal to "ZZZZZ", the solution will continue to loop.

7. In the housekeeping procedure, two files must be opened, each one with a different file number. You may recall from Chapter 3 in this textbook that a file can be assigned any integer from 1 to 255. In this solution, however, there is no reason not to use 1 and 2. Enter the following two lines in the **housekeeping** procedure:

```
FileOpen(1, "EASTFILE.txt", OpenMode.Input)
FileOpen(2, "WESTFILE.txt", OpenMode.Input)
```

8. The finishUp procedure is next. It is placed directly following the housekeeping procedure because both procedures deal with the opening and closing of files. Procedures can be placed in any order in the code. Their location has no effect on how the solution runs. Enter the following two lines in the **finishUp** procedure.

```
FileClose(1)
FileClose(2)
```

9. In the **mainLoop** procedure, there are three remarks to indicate the three tasks that must be accomplished. First, you will write the code that obtains a name for the East variable. Under the **'handle East variable** remark, code the following:

```
If strEastName = Nothing Then
    If EOF(1) Then
        strEastName = "ZZZZZ"
```

```
    Else
        Input(1, strEastName)
    End If
End If
```

10. Coding for the West variable is practically identical. Just change the variable name and the file number. Under the **'handle West variable** remark, code the following:

```
If strWestName = Nothing Then
    If EOF(2) Then
        strWestName = "ZZZZZ"
    Else
        Input(2, strWestName)
    End If
End If
```

11. Once the variables have their appropriate values, they can be compared. If both variables have a value of "ZZZZZ", the merge is complete, and the solution can quit. That is what `Exit Sub` does in the following code block. Otherwise, the two names are compared, and the lower value is added to the list box, as described earlier. Beneath the **'compare names** remark, code the following:

```
If strEastName = "ZZZZZ" And strWestName = "ZZZZZ" Then
    Exit Sub
Else
    If strEastName < strWestName Then
        lstDisplay.Items.Add(strEastName)
        strEastName = Nothing
    Else
        lstDisplay.Items.Add(strWestName)
        strWestName = Nothing
    End If
End If
```

12. Run your solution. Your list box should show ten names in alphabetical order, from "Abel" through "Johnson."

SAVING MERGED DATA

If you can successfully merge two files to a single list box, as you did in the previous activity, sending the merged data to a file is a simple matter. Work through the following steps to save your merged data to a new file in the **bin** folder.

1. In the **housekeeping** procedure, under the two **FileOpen** lines you previously coded, enter the following line: **FileOpen(3, "MERGEDATA.txt", OpenMode.Output)**

2. In the **finishUp** procedure, under your two **FileClose** lines, enter the following line: **FileClose(3)**

3. In the **mainLoop** procedure under the **'compare names** remark, enter the following two **Write** lines that are shown in **bold type**. The lines of code that you previously entered are shown here in *italic type*. Do not type them again.

```
If strEastName < strWestName Then
      lstDisplay.Items.Add(strEastName)
      Write(3, strEastName)
      strEastName = Nothing
Else
      lstDisplay.Items.Add(strWestName)
      Write(3, strWestName)
      strWestName = Nothing
End If
```

4. Run your solution.

5. To examine the file you just created, open your **Merge** folder, open the **bin** folder that it contains, and then double-click **MERGEDATA**. It will open it in Notepad.

6. Your file should look like that shown in Figure 9-2. Exit Notepad, close your solution, and exit VB .NET.

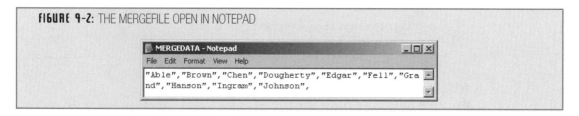

FIGURE 9-2: THE MERGEFILE OPEN IN NOTEPAD

Notice that the strings are enclosed in quotation marks and the comma is the field delimiter.

CHAPTER SUMMARY

In this chapter, you merged two files and displayed the results in a list box. Then you created a new file to store the merged records. The following key points were presented:

- ❏ When VB .NET writes to a sequential file, it encloses text data (strings) in quotation marks. It writes numerical data without quotation marks, and it uses commas, not carriage, returns as delimiters.

- ❏ Whether a solution is reading from or writing to a file, the file must be opened with a file number, which can be any integer from 1 through 255.

- ❏ To read from a file use the `Input` keyword. To write to a file, use the `Write` keyword.

- ❏ Opening a file for output is a destructive operation; that is, any data that the file previously contained is destroyed when the file is opened for output.

- ❏ In order for files to be merged, they must have the same data structure, and they must be sorted the same way.

REVIEW QUESTIONS

Select the best answer to complete each sentence.

1. **To input information from a sequential file use the word _____.**
   a. input
   b. read
   c. get
   d. fetch

2. **To output information to a sequential file use the word _____.**
   a. output
   b. write
   c. put
   d. release

3. **The correct syntax for creating a new sequential file called MYSTUFF is _____.**
   a. `Open "MYSTUFF.txt" for Output As #1`
   b. `FileOpen(2, MYSTUFF.txt, OpenMode.Output)`
   c. `Open (3, "MYSTUFF.txt", OpenMode.Output)`
   d. `FileOpen(4, "MYSTUFF.txt", OpenMode.Output)`

4. **What is meant by the sentence, *Opening a file for output is a destructive operation*?**
   a. If the file is not opened correctly, the solution will crash.
   b. If the data is not output all at once, it will not be successfully saved.
   c. Previously stored data in the file is destroyed as soon as the file is opened.
   d. Previously stored data in the file is erased as soon as new data is placed in the file.

5. **The correct syntax for outputting the word "Lima" to a sequential file is _____.**

   a. `Output (3, "Lima")`
   b. `Write (3, "Lima")`
   c. `WriteLine (3, Lima)`
   d. `Write 3 ("Lima")`

6. **What is wrong with the following block of code?**

   ```
   FileOpen(1, "FILE1.txt", OpenMode.Input)
   FileOpen(1, "FILE2.txt", OpenMode.Input)
   ```

   a. The same file number is used for both files.
   b. Numbers cannot be used in a file name.
   c. Both files are open for Input.
   d. There should be a space between "File" and "Open".

EXERCISES

1. **MakeFile**

   In this exercise, you will use VB .NET to create and write data to a file.

   a. Duplicate the **Inc MakeFile** folder that is inside the **ch09** folder in your student files.
   b. Rename the duplicated folder from **Copy of Inc MakeFile** to **MakeFile**, and then open the solution.
   c. Click **Form1.vb** in the **Solution Explorer** window, then click the **View** menu, and then click **Designer**. Notice that the form contains no objects.
   d. Click the **View** menu, and then click **Code**.
   e. Write one line of code under the '**open file** remark, one line under the '**write data** remark, and one line under the '**close file** remark, so that your three-line solution creates a new sequential file named **WORDFILE.txt** and outputs the word "India" to the file.
   f. Run the solution. When you see the message **all done**, click **OK**, and the solution will stop.
   g. Examine your file in Notepad. You should see the word "India" in quotation marks and followed by a comma.

2. **NumberMerger**

   In this exercise, you will merge two lists of numbers and display the result in a list box. The partially completed solution contains 11 lines, or parts of lines, marked (fill in the code). Replace these with the correct code to display the single, merged list shown in Figure 9-3.

   a. Open the **Inc NumberMerger** folder that is inside the **ch09** folder in your student files.
   b. Open the **bin** folder that is inside the **Inc NumberMerger** folder, and then examine the two sequential files it contains, named **NUM1** and **NUM2**. Notice that the numbers in both files are decimals and are in numerical order.
   c. Duplicate the **Inc NumberMerger** folder, and then rename the duplicate from **Copy of Inc NumberMerger** to **NumberMerger**.
   d. Open **NumberMerger** and examine the code in the **mainLoop**.

e. Under the **'handle NUM2 variable** remark, replace the seven lines that read **(fill in the code)** with the correct code. Use the code under the **'handle NUM1 variable** remark as a model.

f. Under the **'compare numbers** remark, replace the four areas that read **(fill in the code)** with the correct code to complete the merge. Use the code from your completed **Merge** solution as a model, but remember that you are dealing with numbers and not with strings.

g. Run your solution. The list box should look like the one shown in Figure 9-3.

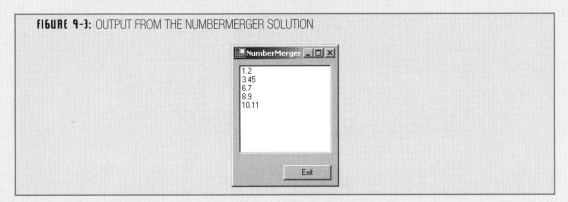

FIGURE 9-3: OUTPUT FROM THE NUMBERMERGER SOLUTION

APPENDIX A

DUPLICATING A SOLUTION FOLDER

Although the following instructions pertain to duplicating a VB .NET solution folder, they can be used to duplicate any Windows folder. The steps that follow describe a technique that uses Copy & Paste from the Edit menu, but if you know how to use the buttons on the standard toolbar or keyboard shortcuts, they will work equally well.

1. Use **Windows Explorer** or browse from the desktop to the folder you wish to copy.
2. Click the folder to select it.
3. Click the **Edit** menu, and then click **Copy**.
4. If you want to keep the duplicate in the same folder as the original, skip this step; otherwise, use Windows Explorer or browse to the location that you want for the duplicated folder.
5. Click the **Edit** menu, and then click **Paste**.

 TIP

If you paste the duplicate in a folder different from the original folder, the two names will remain the same (Figure A-1). However, if you paste the duplicate in the same folder as the original, the name of the duplicate will be changed to "Copy of. . ." (Figure A-2).

FIGURE A-1: ORIGINAL AND DUPLICATE SOLUTION FOLDERS WITHIN DIFFERENT FOLDERS

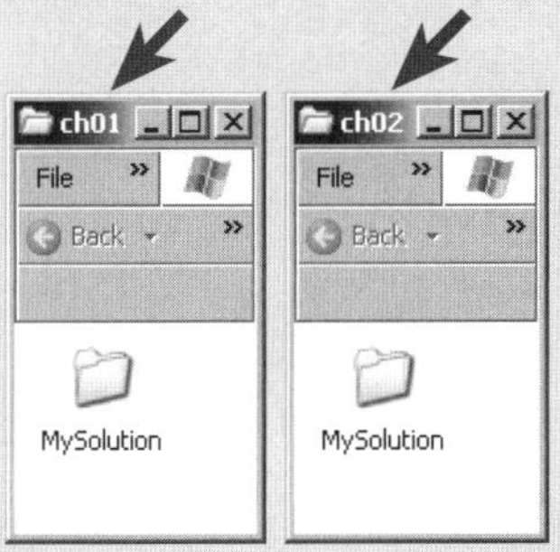

FIGURE A-2: ORIGINAL AND DUPLICATE SOLUTION FOLDERS WITHIN THE SAME FOLDER

APPENDIX B

PRINTING A FORM

Although the following instructions pertain to printing a run-time form in VB .NET, they can be used to print any window in any Windows application. The *Alt+PrintScreen* technique that follows will take a snapshot of whatever window is currently active, regardless of whether you are running a VB .NET solution. The snapshot is placed on the Clipboard, and from there, it can be pasted into most kinds of documents.

1. Start your VB .NET solution, and fill in any information on the form that you want printed. You can print either a blank form or a completed form—the technique is identical for both.

 TIP

You have to be in run time to obtain the desired results. If you follow these steps in design time, you will print out not only the form but the whole screen, including the IDE.

2. While holding down the **Alt** key, click the **Print Screen** key (PrtSc), which is generally near the upper-right corner of your keyboard. Alt+PrintScreen will copy the currently active window (your run-time form) to the Clipboard.

3. Exit or minimize VB .NET.

4. Start either **Word**, **WordPad,** or **Paint** (but not Notepad).

5. Click the **Edit** menu, and then click **Paste**. The active window, which was previously copied to the Clipboard, will be pasted into your document.

6. To print, simply click the **File** menu, and then click **Print**, as you would with any document.

7. Close your current application and return to VB .NET.

▮▮▮▮APPENDIX C

STORAGE OF DATA FILES

When a solution from this textbook needs to access a data file, the file is placed in the bin folder of the solution. For example, in Chapter 3, the Inc Plus100 solution needs to access the Five Primes file. Consequently, the Five Primes file can be found in the bin folder that is inside the Inc Plus100 folder that is inside the ch03 folder that is in the student files, as shown in Figure C1.

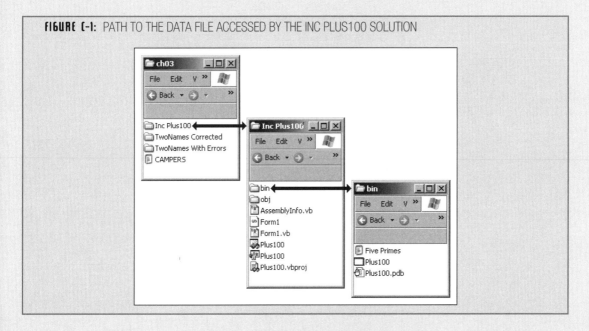

FIGURE C-1: PATH TO THE DATA FILE ACCESSED BY THE INC PLUS100 SOLUTION

The CAMPERS file is also a data file that is needed for an exercise in Chapter 3, but because it is not accessed by the Inc Plus100 solution, it is not placed in the bin folder.

To examine the Five Primes file manually, simply double-click it. The file will open in Notepad. To open it from within a solution, use the following syntax: `FileOpen (1, "Five Primes.txt", OpenMode.Input)`. Notice that the file name extension, *.txt* must be included as part of the file name.

If the data files were stored elsewhere, you would have to include the path as well as the file name in the code. For example, if the Five Primes file is in the root directory of a floppy disk, the code would read `FileOpen (1, "A:\Five Primes.txt", OpenMode.Input)`. If, on the other hand, it is in the My Documents folder on the C drive, you would enter `FileOpen(1, "C:\My Documents\Five Primes.txt", OpenMode.Input)`.

APPENDIX D

USING REPORTER TO COMPLETE THE EXERCISES IN THIS TEXTBOOK

Reporter is a utility solution developed by the author to facilitate the creation of reports from text files and print charts. Reporter displays a report on a computer screen and then allows the report to be sent to a printer.

Beginning with Chapter 5, most of the practice activities and exercises in this textbook use Reporter in partial solutions that must be completed by the student. Although each practice activity and exercise has its own uniquely named solution folder, inside that folder, the name of the solution and the project is Reporter. Work through the following steps for every exercise that uses Reporter:

1. The particular practice activity or exercise that you are working on will inform you of what solution folder and data file is to be used.

2. Open the solution folder, open the **bin** folder that it contains, and then double-click the data file that is used in the practice activity or exercise. The file will open in Notepad.

3. Examine the data to discover the number of fields in the file, determine each field's data type, and decide what variable names you will use for the field data.

4. Duplicate the solution folder, and give the duplicated folder a new name by removing the words **Copy of Inc** from the duplicated folder's name. (Example: If the name of the folder is *Inc Payroll Report*, the duplicated folder will be named *Copy of Inc Payroll Report*. In this case, you would change the name of the duplicated folder to *Payroll Report*.)

5. Open your duplicated solution folder, and then double-click either the **Reporter** solution or the **Reporter** project. The solution will open in VB .NET.

6. In the *heading* region at the top of the **Code** window, you will see the solution title. Beneath it, replace the remark **'Your Name** with your own name or your initials, and then replace the remark **'Date** with the current date. (Remember to keep the apostrophes at the beginning of the remarks.)

7. Under the **'declare variables** remark, declare a variable for every field in the data file. In some exercises, this will already have been done, and you can proceed to the next step.

8. In the **finishUp** procedure, under the **'display author name** remark, replace the words "your own name" with your name or your initials. Make sure they are enclosed in quotation marks.

9. Return to Step 2 of the practice activity or exercise you are working through, and follow the instructions there to complete the solution.

When your solution is completed, you can run it and compare your report to that shown or described in the practice activity or exercise. In addition, your instructor has access to the completed solutions for all the practice activities and exercises in this textbook, and your work can be compared to the completed solutions. However, there is frequently more than one way to accomplish a programming task, so your solutions, even if they are perfectly correct, may not match the ones provided.

If desired, your report can be sent to a printer by simply clicking the `Print` button before stopping the solution. The solution's code can be printed out as well. To print out the code, first stop the solution by clicking `Exit`, then click the `File` menu, and then click `Print`.

APPENDIX E

FILE NAME EXTENSIONS

All Windows files have as part of their name a **file name extension**, a "suffix" that determines what application will open when you double-click your file. You may not see it or even know that it exists, but it is present in all file names. For example, if you saved a Word document with the name *Extend*, it would be stored as *Extend.doc*. Similarly, an Excel spreadsheet with the same name would be stored as *Extend.xls*, while a Notepad document would be *Extend.txt*.

File name extensions can be visible or invisible, depending on how Windows is configured on your computer or workstation. In Windows XP, you can find a check box in the View tab of the Folder Options in the Control Panel that will allow file name extensions to be hidden or displayed. Other versions of Windows have a similar way of hiding or displaying file name extensions.

If file name extensions are visible, it is possible to change them, but if you attempt to do so, Windows will warn you, "If you change a file name extension, the file may become unstable." Changing a file name extension frequently yields some bizarre results. For example, if you change a *.doc* extension to *.txt*, your Word document will open in Notepad, and all the Word control codes will be displayed as garbage characters in Notepad. You will get similar results if you change an *.xls* file to *.doc*.

In common practice, when talking about or writing about a file, just the file name is used, and the extension is omitted. This textbook follows that common practice, with one exception: When opening a file in Visual Basic, the extension must be included. For example, if you are to open, say, the *Extend* file manually, this textbook will instruct you to "double-click the Extend file," but if you are writing code, you will be instructed to use *Extend.txt* as the file name. The instructions should be easy enough to follow in the both cases; however, you should realize that *Extend* and *Extend.txt* refer to the same file.

◼◼◼◼◼INDEX

A

accumulator, using, 76–78

adding line spaces in code, 47

addition operator (+), 13

ampersand (&), concatenation operator, 68

AND statements, 56–57

apostrophes (') and code comments, 12

arguments described, using, 44–45

arithmetic operator, combining with equals sign, 45

arrays, using, 76, 81–82

asterisk (*), multiplication operator, 45

averaging program, 42

B

Back button, navigating files and folders, 20

BASIC vs. Visual Basic, 12

break mode of operation described, 6–7

bugs described, 11

button click events, 20

C

calling procedures, 45, 46

carriage returns
  and code modules, 32
  in data files, 20

case selection code block, 80

case structures, using, 58–59, 78–80

changing
  See also modifying
  data types, 14
  file name extensions, E-105
  text files in Notebook, 20

chapter summaries
  exploring arrays, 83

exploring loops, 73
  getting started, 8
  making decisions, 61
  merging sequential files, 93
  modifying solutions, 16
  modularizing solutions, 49
  reading files, 38
  reading records, 28

character data type, 14, 35

Clipboard, pasting and copying screen shots, B-99

closing programs, Exit button, 37

COBOL vs. Visual Basic, 12

code
  comments, 12
  commas and carriage returns, 32
  debugging. *See* debugging
  examining in Code window, 12
  hiding and displaying hidden, 46–48
  indenting, 54
  line spaces, adding to, 47
  loops described, 67
  modularization of, 12
  obtaining hardcopy of, 15
  parentheses in, 45
  remarks in, 12
  understanding corrected TwoNames, 26–27
  variable declarations, 12

Code window
  described, using, 4, 6
  opening, 11

coding
  merging of files, 90
  modularized solutions, 42
  AND operators, 56–57
  OR operators, 57–58

commands, different methods for, 3

commas (,)
  and code modules, 32
  delimiters, 33, 86

comments in code, 12

comparing names in files, 91

concatenating described, 68

controls described, 6

copying
  See also duplicating
  folders, 10

counters
  and accumulators, 76–78
  displaying value of, 68

creating
  label maker, 70
  procedures, 37
  report using case structure, 78–80
  text files in Notebook, 20

currency
  data type, 14
  fields representing, 33
  FormatCurrency function, 46

cutting and pasting procedures, 24

D

data
  files and storage, C-101
  input and output, sequential files, 86
  processing and displaying results, 55
  saving merged, 91
  writing to files, 88

data-processing paradigm, logical flowchart (fig.), 32

data types
  changing, 14
  of variables, 13, 35